The Second Meanest Man in the World

(is not)

Bryan Johnston

(he's the author)

This book is dedicated to Bob Newman.

Gertrude, Boris S. Wort, Ggoorrsstt
Leroy Frump, Miss Smith, The Swami, Paddy Wagon
Ketchikan, Charlie Can Do, Sturdly
Dingbatman, Mr. X. R. Cise

"People in Seattle are always so polite, which makes me feel like I always have to be polite as well. That is so rude."

(Overheard in a Capitol Hill Starbucks)

The night was dark. Darker than the inside of a cow, as they might say in Arkansas, or other places that even people from Arkansas make fun of. Like Kent or Lynnwood. It was a night for skinny vanilla lattes, 155 degrees, with six pumps of caramel sauce, plus cinnamon dolce and whipped cream. And wearing socks with sandals. And avoiding eye-contact with strangers. In other words, just another night in Seattle.

Except it wasn't just another night. The incident two tables to my left was my first inkling something was amiss. The players were as follows: Edgy looking male 20-something anti-hipster with ripped jeans and wallet chain and his doe-eyed female companion in yoga pants and ironic boy scout shirt. On their table, two cups, and nothing else. The anti-hipster dude stood up, and I kid you not, yelled, (yelled!) "I now pronounce you dumped and single! You may now kiss my ass!" At which point he stormed out of the coffee shop without even picking up his Grande.

I'm sure I don't have to tell you how many red flags we've got here. For one, neither of the couple had a laptop with them. Weird in and of itself. Two, the kid that stormed out didn't bother to drop his cup in the recycle bin. But the most glaring issue was that this type of behavior simply doesn't take place in a Seattle Starbucks. At most you'd get a muted disagreement and lots of staring at the tabletop which would end with the couple leaving together after they brushed off the table of any stray biscotti crumbs. That's just the Seattle way. I should know, I've been writing about it my entire adult life. Chances are you've read my column, *Sooo Seattle*, three days a week in one of Seattle's always-on-life-support print mediums. Ten years at the PI, until that place got chloroformed. Eight years at the venerable Times, until they went the way of the Mazda rotary engine. Most recently at the area's latest fish wrap, the aptly and non-ironically named The Analog. Once the Times closed-up shop, an anonymous bazillionaire with more dough than brains (but a sense of humor) stepped in and started up his own paper, God love him. For the life of me, I can't figure out why. Maybe he's got some strange affinity for Saint Jude, the patron of lost causes and hopeless cases. The dude probably still has a Palm Pilot and a fax machine. Not that I'm complaining. Hey, if he's willing to cut me a bi-weekly check I'm not about to bite the hand. Clearly, the man's a romantic.

I was destined to write my column. A born and bred Seattleite, I know this town better than anyone I know. I can actually tell you the difference between Pike and Pine. I was at Mariners/Yankees game 5 for Junior's mad dash. I was using the term Keep Clam before Ivar stole it for purely mercenary purposes. I rode the Bubbleator; I ate at Dag's; I still eat at Dick's. The Ye Olde Curiosity Shop was a childhood visitation staple, as was Jones' Fantastic Museum in the basement of the Seattle Center (Come see Olaf the Giant!). I watched The Count on Nightmare Theater and have swum in Green Lake without getting sick. I can proudly state that I never once visited Tubs, the hot-tub-rental-by-the-hour establishment in the U-district (How anyone could and not contract some latent deadly infection is beyond me). I still call Macy's The Bon; I bought vinyl at Tower Records; I listened to Emperor Smith when KJR rocked, and watched Star Wars at the UA 150.

And my name just adds to the resume. My parents, Lois and William Street, clearly must have known what my future would hold from the moment I was born, if what they put on my birth certificate was any indication. Ol' Lois and Bill must have thought it a hoot to name their only son Stewart. Yes, that's my name, Stewart Street. Laugh it up.

I get this town. I get it like Ron Jeremy gets monthly testing. So, when the Starbucks Incident unfolded (so shall it be called, henceforth) my Seattle antenna gave a little twitch. Within a few weeks the twitch had grown to full blown vibrations. Not long after the Starbucks Incident, I witnessed a pedestrian cross a street before it said Walk. Helllloooo, this is Seattle. Polite capital of the world. Well, maybe second to Canada, but still! We say please and thank you around here, dammit. Hey, I get the whole Seattle Freeze thing (Have a nice day. Somewhere else.) but at least we're considerate about it. All I know is that something fishy was going on. There was clearly a disturbance in Seattle's Force. Our vibe was out of whack, and I was going to find out why.

One of the beauties of writing for a paper is that over the years you put together a pretty healthy Rolodex—excuse me, database. I had connections all over town and it was time to start putting out feelers. My first call was to a character whom I've worked with in the past. The guy seemed to have his finger on the pulse of everything that happened in the city. He was clearly connected, but you'd never know it at first blush. He wore a white suit and rumpled straw hat with a black band. Whenever he spoke he would steeple his fingers together in front of him and he had the most ridiculous mustache imaginable. It was undeniably Fu Manchu-ish, like two long pieces of black yarn bracketing his mouth. And when he spoke he sounded like some white guy trying to do an over-the-top, stereotyped Chinese accent. In this day and age, it would come across racist as hell if that wasn't the way the dude actually spoke. I once asked him what he thought of Mickey Rooney's portrayal of Mr. Yunoshi in Breakfast at Tiffany's. His answer? "Nailed it." I let it drop after that. The dude was weird, but in my experience, nobody could help me get to the bottom of this quicker than the man in the white suit—Charlie Can Do, number one detective. The name fit; he simply had a knack for tracking stuff down. Granted, his strange, almost Zen-like demeanor gave me the creeps but I can't argue with his success.

From what I've been able to divine, Charlie came to the States as a teenager. What year is beyond my reckoning. After working my sources in Chinatown, I learned that even as a young man he was naturally inquisitive. He was always asking questions, sticking his nose where it didn't belong. As a result, he constantly found himself on the short end of short-tempered people who didn't like so many questions being asked. Apparently, this only drove Charlie even more to keep up his snooping. You won't find Charlie on Google when searching for private investigators, but clearly the man is in high demand. As for the white suit getup, the funky Fu Manchu, and ridiculous accent, your guess is as good as mine. Everyone's got a calling card, and he's certainly got the goods on that account.

I called him up and he agreed to meet me at the Comet Tavern on Capitol Hill. Not even Charlie stood out in that place.

The Comet is a bar's kind of bar, located at 9th and Pike (not Pine), the joint has been getting people drunk for over 80 years. It's a helluva lot nicer than it was back in the day, but it's still got the Seattle vibe baked into its walls. I grabbed a seat under the giant neon C along the wall and watched assorted Millenniums shoot lousy pool and heft bottles of Hamm's and Rainier. While I nursed an Olympia, and threw back a handful of hot nuts, a voice appeared just over my shoulder.

"Ah, Missah Street. We meet again."

I turned to see the impeccably dressed Charlie standing before me. His suit—the only one I've ever seen him, by my eye—as pure as the driven snow. His dry-cleaning bill must be nuts. I motioned to the chair across from me and he eased into the seat with more grace than I've exhibited in my entire lifetime.

"Hey, Chuck, good to see you." He responded with a simple nod. He never did like being called Chuck, but what the hell, I get my kicks where I can. "Look, I'll cut to the chase, something's funky in Jet City and I figured you might be in the know."

Can Do tipped his head to the side like a dog who still hasn't quite figured out human speech and raised a pencil-thin eyebrow that would have made

Marlene Dietrich proud. Then with a slow nod, "Ah so."

I quickly glanced around. "Jeezus, will you knock it off with the Ah so crap; someone's going to pop you one."

Charlie simply nodded thoughtfully. "Whata is it you feel isa wrong?" Think a Chinese version of Jar Jar Binks. I shared with him my concerns while he patiently listened. I told him about the jaywalker episode and he responded with a sideways glance and a subtle roll of his fingers on the table—the equivalent of anyone else jumping to their feet and screaming in shocked disbelief. I'd clearly gotten to him. He held a finger in the air and proclaimed, "Confucius say, man who run before bus get tired, but man who run behind bus get exhausted."

I waited on that for a moment, expecting further explanation. After a lengthy pause, I realized I wasn't going to get one. "What the hell does that mean?"

Can Do smiled, nodded and threw out another utterly profound, and equally cryptic quote. "Confucius say, two wrongs not make a right, but two rights make a U-turn."

That's what you got with Charlie, deep thoughts, weird-ass observations and a whole lot of Confucius-isms. In all my dealings with him not one of his Far East quotes has ever made a lick of sense to me, but whatever, it's all part of the Charlie

Can Do package. You put up with it to get the rest of him, and the rest usually brings results.

It took me three Oly's and two bowls of hot nuts to run through all my thoughts and observations. When I wrapped up, he elegantly rose from his chair, tipped his hat, told me he would be in touch and drifted out the door like a dry-cleaning bag on a soft breeze.

There are a handful of women who are famous enough to go simply by one name: Madonna, Cher, Rihanna, Enya, Charo, Divine. In Seattle, it's Gertrude. Seattle has had its share of famous women, but few are more deeply ingrained into the community's culture than she of the bright red smile.

Gertrude has become nothing short of a local celebrity around these parts. Which is saying something for a telephone operator. Even her standard line to hold while she puts a call through—"One-moment plee-ease," (upping the pitch on the PLEE)—has become a catch phrase with the younger set. I'll hear it out on the Ave in the U district or on Broadway on Cap Hill. A kid will ask their buddy how they're doing and the buddy responds by holding his hand up to his ear in the hang-loose sign, like it's a phone—"One-moment plee-ease"—before yucking it up. When you meet Gertrude herself, I gotta say, she's something to behold. The frock, the Raggedy Ann hair, the crown, those army boots! The woman cuts as fine a figure as you're likely to see. A little heavy on the makeup, but that's like quibbling about the steering wheel cover in a Ferrari. They don't give out the title, Miss City Dump, purely on congeniality.

Although there was a bit of a brew-ha-ha when she was crowned. Whispers of undue influence, back room dealings swirled for weeks. And totally understandable. I mean, she's the main squeeze of the mayor of the city dump, so, naturally, people are going to talk. But at the same time, honestly, the moment you lay eyes on her, how can you deny her the crown? She's a woman among girls.

Any guy in town would give his eye teeth to be on the arm of Gertrude, but I'll put my own girl against her any day of the week and twice on Sundays. Her name is Astrid Strom, a gorgeous little Ballard Norskie who takes no guff and keeps me on the straight and narrow. She's what is commonly referred to as a dark Norwegian, which means she's not blonde and blue-eyed. She's run-of-the-mill brunette, and has the spectacular ability to tan like a mother, without an ounce of Coppertone. As a result, by August she more resembles someone south of the equator than Nordic. Like myself, Astrid works at the paper, news beat. The woman has a Rolodex to kill for. We met way-back-when at the Dog House, a smoky piano bar in the Denny Triangle that folded up in 1994, which in turn changed over to the Hurricane, which eventually changed over to who-the-hell-knows. I lost interest. But in my salad days the Dog House was a damn cool place to stagger home from. Quick history lesson: It was originally located a block away at 7th and Denny (now a Déjà vu strip club), strategically located at the southern end of the Aurora Speedway. Speedway being relative. You could reach speeds of 30 mph! The Dog House flourished until the city built the Battery Street Tunnel. People no longer had to bail out at Denny, and thus, the Dog House. But the plucky joint stuck around for another 40-odd-years. I was never a smoker myself but after spending a night wearing out the great American songbook with the piano man you basically inhaled the equivalent of two packs of Camel Reds. By my math, the Dog House probably shortened my life-span by a good five years. No complaints from me.

But I digress. Not only did Astrid make a damn fine lefse, but she was also a news gathering machine. She was my next stop. It was after nine so I knew just where to find her. I jumped in my rig and made a beeline for Ballard. Crossing the Ballard bridge, I was greeted with the warm red glow of a giant neon sign off to the right, offering the gentle suggestion to Add Bardahl. Whenever I see that sign my mind immediately goes through a cool Seafair flashback domino effect. I see the Bardahl sign, I think of the Miss Bardahl hydro—the cool one with the yellow and black checkerboard—which then makes me think of about two decades of other hydros from my youth: The Miss Budweiser, Pride of Pay N Pak, Notre Dame (with the clover on the tail), Atlas Van Lines, Miss Madison, the patriotic looking Miss Vans PX, Lincoln Thrift, Circus Circus, The Squire Shop, Pizza Pete, fire engine red Miss Timex, and of course, the only boat sponsored by a local rock band, Barney Armstrong's Machine! My mind then hopscotches down memory lane to me riding my Schwinn Sting Ray one-speed, complete with banana seat, flying-V handlebars and sissy bar, dragging a wooden model hydro (Sometimes the Bud, sometimes Miss Timex). The picture wouldn't be complete without the requisite playing cards clothes pinned into the spokes to sound like an engine.

I take a left off of 15th onto Market Street, the corner where Manning's Cafeteria and Buffet used to inhabit, and moments later I'm keeping a weather eye out for that most rare and elusive beast: an open parking spot in Old Ballard.

Moments later I find Astrid at the prescribed location, tucked into a booth at Hattie's Hat, nursing an Old Fashioned and slowly working her way through a dog-eared copy of Sherman Alexie's Smoke Signals.

"Street," she said, without even looking up.

"Hey, Punkin'," I replied. I looked around the dark room. "You know, one of these days we're going to eat at Canlis."

"Can't afford it."

It was our running gag. Our ratio of eating out versus eating at home was around ten to one. I'm vaguely aware that there's an oven in my apartment. I'm also aware that when we do eat out it's not at locations of the four-star variety. Canlis, being of that variety. I slid into her booth. "I need your help."

She quietly set a dollar bill in the book to mark her place and gave me her full attention, a quality I envied tremendously, being that I have the attention span of a five-year-old. "'Sup?"

"Any stories lately that caught your attention?"

"What do you mean?"

"You know, anything that struck you as unusual or out of the ordinary?"

She leaned back and looked up at the ceiling, biting her lip as she is wont to do when she's rolling the marbles around in her head. "Now that you mention it, I got a tip on something that gave me pause. Over at the Bongo Congo Kennels; the animal man's been a busy boy."

"Ketchikan?" Ketchikan the Animal Man was known by everyone within the Puget Sound area as THE resident zoology expert. And to top it off, his wardrobe kicked ass. A pith helmet, shoulder epaulets; the man's professional countenance basically screamed professional competence. And did he know how to make an entrance. Every time he made an appearance it was to the sound of a march ("Our Director" by Frederick Ellsworth Bigelow, to be exact), which could be started and stopped by tapping the crown of his hat.

"He's been making an over-abundance of house calls to the city dump."

"J.P.'s dog, Griswald taken ill?"

"Nope."

"Guardian Elephant?"

"Nope."

"Topakity Bird?"

"Keep trying."

I mentally scrolled through every animal that resided at the dump. The list was getting short. "Uh, Morgan the Frog?"

"Give up?"

"I give. Uncle."

"Think Blue Swede's Hooked on a Feeling."

"The frpl?" I didn't see that coming. "Ketchikan has been seeing Ggoorrsstt? Why?"

"Dunno. My source didn't say. Just said Ketchikan's been wearing out the dump's Dutch-door."

The plot thickened. A peck on the cheek and I was out the door.

I needed to clear my head and crank up the endorphins, so I headed to the gym to release a little lactic acid. My gym of choice was a little known, and lesser used hole in the wall in Fremont run by an old geezer who clearly wasn't familiar with the term disinfectant. Bare, squalid and utterly no-nonsense, it was the kind of place that still had Indian Clubs—those weird wooden things that look like bowling pins. I found the usual cast of characters going through their constitutionals—one guy was killing himself doing burpees, another was lifting absurd amounts of pot metal, while an out-of-place looking 20-something goth chick was pounding out an impressive beat with a jump rope. You normally didn't find more than a half-dozen people in here at any one time. It wasn't the type of place that got busy on January first with New Year's resolutioners. I often wondered how the owner managed to keep the lights on, but guessing that he'd been here since Hector was a pup, I'd wager the mortgage was long settled. Word on the street was that he opened the joint after making his fortune as J.P. Patches' personal fitness guru, back before anyone had heard of spandex. Speaking of the owner, I saw him over by the rack of free weights. For an old timer, he still cut an impressive figure. I couldn't tell you his real name but everybody knew him as Mr. X. R. Cize. He wore a white jumpsuit and black rimmed glasses. He sported a tiny, pencil-thin mustache that looked like an inverted V sitting on his upper lip, and his shock of curly blonde hair had long since gone white. But the man could still pump some serious iron.

I saddled up next to Mr. Cize when he was between sets. "Hey, X. R. What's the haps?"

"Arm day."

I glanced at his impressive guns and simply nodded. I don't choose my daily haunts just for the atmosphere; every place, every person is a source, and they each have a finger on the pulse of all things Seattle. I carefully dipped my toe in the water to see what I might find. "You feeling chatty today?"

Cize started a new set, never braking his slow arm-pumping rhythm. "Depends. What's the subject?"

"The Animal Man."

The old man broke the tiniest of smiles. "I might."

"What do you know?"

He stopped in mid-curl and turned a bemused smile on me. "Twenty push-ups and I'll tell you."

"Seriously? You're not going to tell me anything unless I do twenty push-ups?"

"You've been looking a little flabby lately, Street. It'll do you good."

He was just busting my chops with the flabby line. I've always been on the narrow side, and I'm a sports nut, so I've spent more than my share of hours on the field, court or in the gym. Still doesn't mean I like doing push-ups.

"Twenty push-ups? That's extortion!"

"Twenty-five."

"Twenty-five! I'm lucky to push myself out of bed in the morning!"

Cize just went on with his curls and paid me no mind. I stood there fuming for a moment before I finally caved and dropped to the floor. I knew I could do twenty-five push-ups, and he knew I could do twenty-five push-ups, but I played along with the charade. I puffed, grunted and groaned for effect before slowly climbing to my feet. "All right, give."

Cize finished his set and carefully re-racked the weights. "So, I was out with Gertrude and J.P. a few weeks back. A late dinner at 13 Coins, but before the poseurs show up."

I nodded; I knew the drill. After a certain hour, the millennials start creeping in, with their yoga pants and Uggs, or beards and rolled up cuffs, ordering Tanqueray and tonics and leaving 5% tips. Of course, I shouldn't complain, I was one of those dorks half a lifetime earlier. Cize went on with his story.

"As per usual, Gertrude was the center of attention, all laughs and loudness. Nothing out of the ordinary until our after-dinner drinks. While Gertrude sipped a Frangelico and coffee she made a comment that caught my attention. She said she had a strange run-in the previous week. She says she was down at Uwajimaya, doing some shopping, when she heard cackling from the next aisle."

"Cackling. The only people that cackle are witches."

"Correct."

"And the only working witch around these parts is…"

"Right. Zenobia. (gasp)"

I gasped too, because that's what you do when you hear Zenobia's name. "Zenobia (gasp) shops at Uwajimaya? She taking a Szechuan cooking class?"

"Don't know. Gertrude says she peered through a gap in a stack of wasabi jars and there was Zenobia (gasp) in all her glory, filling up a shopping cart with all sorts of exotic herbs."

This was indeed peculiar. Zenobia (gasp) wasn't known for leaving her castle for run-of-the-mill trips to Fred Meyers and Albertsons. The fact that she was down amongst the rabble (as she saw it) was one thing, but that she was stocking up at Uwajimaya was something else entirely. Clearly, she was up to mischief. I asked, "Did Zenobia (gasp) know Gertrude saw her?"

"Doesn't sound like it. Gertrude said she watched her for a bit before her curiosity wore off and she shuffled off to stock up on crème rinse. Apparently though, the run-in stuck with Gertrude, because she said it's been nagging at her ever since. I've never seen Gertrude like that. Usually the only thing that Gertrude is concerned about is Gertrude."

I couldn't argue with that. The woman was dynamite, but they didn't come more self-centered. "Okay, so back to my question. Have you heard anything about Ketchikan?"

Cize nodded and leaned in conspiratorially. "Here's where it gets weird. While we're sipping our aperitifs, J.P. gets up to take a powder. The minute he's out of earshot Gertrude tells me she's worried about Ggoorrsstt. She says he's been acting very strangely lately. Grumpy. Angry. Definitely not   himself."

"Why did she wait until J.P. was out of the room to tell you?"

"My question exactly. She says she's brought it up to him but he didn't seem to think there was a problem. In fact, she even said that J.P. himself had been acting a bit surly."

At this, my antenna really started quivering. The Clown was never surly. He was a clown for crying out loud! Clearly the shock that I felt was showing on my face.

"Yep, that's the same reaction I had," said Cize.

"How was J.P. acting that evening at dinner?"

"Like normal. Cracking jokes, doing the Patches Chuckle. He was having a ball. I didn't see anything out of the ordinary, and I said as much to Gertrude."

"What did she say to that?"

"She said, that's why she wasn't saying anything while he was at the table. She said he was generally his normal self, but every now and then she saw something in his behavior that struck her as out of character. He'd glare at Grandpa Tick-Tock when the water would spit out of the clock on him to wake him up; he snapped at Sturdly after the bookworm chewed up one of his Clown Illustrated magazines."

"Probably the swimsuit issue," I replied.

"Yeah, maybe. Still, peculiar for J.P., nonetheless."

"So, again, what does this have to do with Ketchikan?"

"Gertrude said since J.P. didn't seem to think there was anything to worry about with Ggoorrsstt she took it upon herself to contact the Animal Man. She said she would meet him down at the city dump and let him into the secret room so he could check out the frple himself."

"What's he think?"

"At this point, Gertrude says Ketchikan has no idea."

"But apparently, he's still making late night house calls."

"Yep."

So, I now had confirmation on Astrid's source's info. The frple was ill, Ketchikan was on the case, and the diagnosis was non-conclusive. I knew where my next stop would be. The Bongo Congo Kennels. The Animal Man and I needed to have a chat.

But first I had a date with the squat rack. Leg day.

The Bongo Congo Kennel is more than a kennel. A kennel suggests it's a place simply for dogs and cats. Au contraire. The Bongo Congo is closer to Noah's Ark. At any one time, you can find among the expected puppies and kitties, an assortment of countless other wildlife: wolverines, snakes, orangutans, you name it. And they are all named Fred. Animal Man humor, I guess.

Ketchikan rose to local stardom during the animal hey-days of the 60s. With the likes of Marlin Perkins on television's Mutual of Omaha's Wild Kingdom, Clarence the cross-eyed lion on Daktari, Gentle Ben and Flipper, anything or anybody related to the furry, finned or feathered was held in high esteem. Ketchikan became a staple on J.P.'s TV show and before long the Animal Man's fame took off. The event that really put him over the top didn't even have to do with anything animal related, at least not real animals. When J.P. was out of town, Ketchikan was frequently asked to run the show for him. On one of those shows Ketchikan became famous for doing nothing more than trying to read a children's story. It was Henny Penny. Apparently saying Henny Penny, Ducky Daddles, Cockey Lockey, Turkey Lurkey and Goosey Poosey over and over was too much for the Animal Man and he quite literally fell off his stool laughing. Uncontrollably. If YouTube had existed in those days he would have become an Internet sensation. Even without YouTube, that televised moment made Ketchikan even more lovable than ever. Who doesn't like a good laugh?

I found Ketchikan fussing over an enormous badger. For all intents and purposes it sounded like they were having a conversation. The badger gave a short, guttural grunt, followed by a chattering sound. Bob answered in kind. When the badger noticed me it gave a dismissive snort and turned away, but not before Ketchikan got in a quick muzzle rub. As the badger waddled away, much more gracefully than you would have imagined, the Animal Man waved at the beast in farewell, "See ya, Fred. We'll talk more later."

As I walked over he rose to his feet and met me half way with an outstretched hand.

I gave him my best smile. "Dr. Doolittle, I presume?"

As we shook he nodded over his shoulder at the departing badger, "Ain't she a peach? From out in Minnesota. Paw trouble. Should be good to go within the week."

"She? Fred's a girl."

"And no finer one you'll find. Badgers get a bad rap for being ferocious but she's been nothing but a complete and utter sweetheart since she's been here.

24

I'm going to miss her." Ketchikan turned and headed back to his chair and dropped in. "Street, isn't it? Reporter? I've read your stuff."

I shrugged. "Columnist, technically, but a reporter today."

Ketchikan has always been a larger than life character, gregarious to a fault. He smiled broadly and motioned me to a chair opposite him. "So, what brings you to the Bongo Congo Kennel? A story on animal adoption? Care and feeding of albino anacondas? Speak, lad!"

"I come seeking information on an even rarer species. Frples."

This clearly caught the Animal Man by surprise but he quickly regained his composure. "Fascinating creatures, frples. Happy as the day is long."

"One might also describe them as…friendly," I offered.

Ketchikan smiled broadly and wagged a finger at me. "One might."

I slipped a little deeper into reporter mode. "But word on the street is that our resident frple hasn't been so friendly lately. I thought you might be able to tell me something about that."

Ketchikan sank a bit deeper into his chair and rested his clasped hands in his lap. I waited out a pregnant pause and could tell he was weighing how much to tell me. "Word on the street is reasonably accurate. But I'm not too concerned. My guess is that he just got some bad frple fodder."

"Wait, bad frple fodder? Where exactly do you get frple fodder? I'm guessing you can't just pick up a bag at the local Mud Bay."

Ketchikan shook his head. "No, there are only two places to get frple fodder around these parts—farmer Fred from Fife or farmer Frank from Ferndale. And it has to be fresh; frples are notoriously picky eaters. On rare occasions, usually a special birthday treat, our resident frple will get foreign fantastique fodder from farmer Francois in France."

The resident frple he's talking about is none other than Ggoorrsstt the friendly frple, who lives down at the city dump with J.P. Patches.

Frple's are an odd-looking beast. They're furry, man-sized critters, light brown in color. They have one big oval eye, a single eyebrow and two black antennae. Oh yeah, and their feet are shaped like scuba flippers. Frples are not native to the Pacific Northwest; they can be found on the island of ORIK, near the sister islands of OMOK and GNIK. But somehow one found its way here and was taken in and cared for by J.P.

"What's your interest in Ggoorrsstt?" asked Ketchikan.

I told him how I was noticing odd behavior by the local inhabitants, and found it coincidental that the frple was exhibiting similar behavior.

"Well, frple DNA isn't far removed from humans, so it is possible that they could both suffer from similar afflictions."

I asked if it might be possible to see Ggoorrsstt in person. Ketchikan said he'd check with Ggoorrsstt and J.P. to see if they had any objections and that he'd be in touch.

I gave him a look. "Word on the street is that the Clown isn't aware you're checking in on the frple. A little birdy tells me Gertrude's got you on the case."

Ketchikan gave a clever look and nodded. "Birdies seem to know a lot these days. Okay, it's true, J.P. doesn't know, and he probably doesn't need to. No need to cause alarm when none is necessary. I'll touch base with Gertrude and get back to you."

I took that as my cue to leave, thanked him for his time and headed for the exit, side-stepping a red panda, two bobcats and a wood duck. All named Fred.

I needed to collect my thoughts and feed by gullet so I zipped into Belltown for a date with the 5 Point Café, not to be confused with the 5 Spot up on Queen Anne hill. For the record, you will not leave hungry at either location, but on this occasion, I was craving a good Chicken Fried Steak, and you'll find no finer than at the 5 Point. I also wanted a strong drink, so there was that. The 5 Point's tag line is *Alcoholics serving alcoholics since 1929*. They also boast the title of the "Longest-run family eatery in Seattle," and "Belltown's oldest bar", which is no small feat. I like the joint because it has a checkerboard motif (Miss Bardahl, anyone?) and a periscope in the men's room that offers a lovely view of the Space Needle. What's not to like?

I gave a wave to the Chief Seattle statue standing out front in Tilikum Place and a thumbs up to the neon sign in the window of the Café proudly stating that they've been cheating tourists and drunks since the aforementioned 1929. I found a booth in the bar, ordered my requisite meal and Bloody Mary, and began to piece together the puzzle. By the time I'd polished off my second-round I still wasn't any closer to a brilliant conclusion. I zoned out, chewing on my stick of celery and idly watched the TV up in the corner of the bar. It was a commercial for yoga pants. Like yoga pant retailers need a commercial. Seems like every other woman in Seattle was sporting these Lycra wonders. Even without the audio I got the message loud and clear: *These are not your average, garden variety yoga pants, these are locally made yoga pants, stitched together right here in your backyard!* (Seattleites are suckers for local stuff) *With our within-the-hour* delivery (How is that even possible?) *you can be wearing a pair in no time flat! And with our incredible introductory offer—$10—*(Seriously?) *we're practically giving them away! You've got nothing to lose!*

I actually thought about placing an order for Astrid when I caught sight of a familiar face entering the bar. His dark blue uniform and British Bobby Helmet announced his presence with authority. There are cops, and there are cops. And then there's Officer Paddy Wagon. Nobody messed with the Wagon. The crowd parted like the Red Sea as Paddy strolled through, spinning his old school billy club in that casual manner, developed from decades of idle practice, filling long nights on the beat. He sauntered up to the bar where a space magically opened right before him. A subtle nod to the bartender and in a flash a tumbler of single malt scotch (straight up, natch) appeared before him. He threw down the drink in one swift motion and another, identical glass was already waiting for him on the bar. He picked it up and swept his steely gaze around the room. When he lit on me, a slow smile appeared under his handlebar mustache and he crossed the space in two John Waynish strides.

"Mr. Street," he bellowed above the din with his thick Irish accent. "And what mightcha be doin' in this fair establishment, this fine evenin'?"

"Getting stumped," I said.

"Ah, might I detect a bit of frustration, tinged with the loving warm embrace of our mutual friend, a one Bloody Mary?"

"You would. And it would be two Bloody Marys."

"Ah, 'tis a cruel world that we live in, when even the finest journalists of our day are forced to turn to the devil's crutch to salve their weary minds."

The man did have a way with words. "Finishing your beat?"

"Indeed I am, indeed I am." He raised his glass, gave a nod and sipped his scotch with true appreciation.

"You throw back your first glass like it's rot gut, but your second glass you treat like it's God's own elixir. What gives?"

"Well then, the first glass is a lower brand, still of discerning quality I dare say, but used for the sole purpose of primin' the pump, as it were. But the second glass, faith and begorrah, this is the purpose man was placed on this green earth, don't you know."

He held the glass up to the light like he was gazing upon the Virgin Mary herself. You can't help but respect a man with priorities that squared away.

"So what might be troublin' your soul, Mr. Street?"

I thought about how to answer that but instead decided to, again, do a little fishing. "Paddy, you notice anything peculiar lately? With the daily rank and file? Strange behavior?"

The cop twirled his handlebar and gave me a long look. "And why might you be askin' that, me brother?"

"It's just that I've been seeing things that strike me as odd. I want to know if I'm off my nut, or if there really is something to it."

Paddy took a longer than normal sip and swished the amber liquid around in his mouth like it was a swig of Scope. I could tell he was debating whether to share something with me or not. In the end, he decided sharing was caring. "As a matter of fact, I have." He leaned in and looked around like he was afraid someone might be listening in. "Strange times, indeed, Mr. Street. Strange times."

"What makes you say that, Paddy? What have you seen?"

"Last week, I'm down at Green Lake, don't you know, having a stroll, when I saw something that took me breath away."

"What was it?"

"Runners. Like you might see on any given day. Nothin' out of the ordinary at first, everyone keepin' to the inside lane, as expected. But then…"

He paused and shook his head like he was having a hard time accepting what he saw. "And then I sees a pair of particularly quick runners gaining on a slower pair ahead of them. But instead of yelling, "On your right!" and politely passing, they didn't say a word; they simply ran through the slower couple, and elbowed them aside, like they was fightin' for a 62" flat screen door-buster at Best Buy."

I quite literally gasped at this, almost like someone had just said Zenobia (gasp). "Elbowed them aside. Seriously."

"I've seen a lot in me day, me brother, but the sight of that froze me in me tracks." Paddy shook his head slowly. "And that wasn't the last of it. While I was still tryin' to grasp what I just set me eyes upon, somethin' even more remarkable happened."

"What?" I couldn't imagine something more shocking that what he'd just described.

"It starts rainin'. Nothing special, just a light shower, like you see 300 days a year." He pauses again. Clearly shook. "So what do you think happens next?"

I shrugged. "Nothing."

Paddy hung his head like he'd just drove over a bag of kittens. "The runners…they ran for cover."

I snorted in disbelieve, waiting for Paddy to give up on the joke. Except he didn't. He stared me down, all business. I said, "What do you mean they ran for cover? Maybe you misinterpreted what was happening. Maybe they realized they were late for a spin class or something. Pure coincidence."

Paddy shook his head with the look of a man who's seen more than he bargained for. "No, lad, they ran for cover. Straight under a cedar tree they did. They stood there, debatin' whether to wait out "the storm" or head for their cars. I couldn't believe me eyes or ears."

I took this bombshell in with surprising calm. I wasn't imagining things; something strange was going on. What Paddy just laid before me was shocking: Seattleites showing attitude, and Seattleites being weather wimps. It didn't make any sense. I asked Paddy if maybe the runners weren't local; maybe they were from back east or something. He sadly shook his head. "No lad, they were wearing Brooks running shoes and REI outerwear. No, they were locals, as sure as I'm sittin' here."

After a moment of silence, I told him what I'd seen as well. He agreed with my assessment; something funky was going on in the Emerald City. I asked if he had any suggestions. Paddy thought for a moment and pointed a finger my way. "When things get...unnatural, there's only one person I trust to set me on the right path. The Swami."

This I wasn't expecting. "Of Pastrami?"

"None other," said Paddy.

Seattle's top cop turns to a so-called master of the supernatural for guidance? Never in a million years would I have imagined such a thing.

I fixed him with a jaundiced eye. "What could that wacko offer?"

"Don't you be questionin' things outside of your ken, lad. The Swami has forgotten more than you or I have learned in our lifetimes, combined."

I gave him a look that showed what he was offering was three-day-old fish, and I wasn't buying. "You want me to believe that the Swami of Pastrami might have some valuable insight into what's ailing Seattle? Come on!"

But Paddy didn't budge. "Believe you me, lad, there have been more times than I care to count when the Swami has offered valuable insights that have led to cases bein' broken. And this is off the record, mind you."

"Okay, I'll bite, when did the Swami help out Seattle's finest?"

Paddy looked around again to make sure we weren't being overheard. "Do you promise this information never sees the likes of a single column inch of your darlin' paper?"

I knew the importance of keeping sources secret. "You have my word."

Paddy nodded, accepting my oath. "The Weyerhaeuser kidnappin', Ted Bundy, Green River Killer, Wah Mee Massacre, Mia Zapata Murder, Mary Kay Letourneau…"

"The Swami helped you break all those cases?"

Paddy threw up two hands. "I'm not sayin' he did, but I'm not sayin' he didn't either. I'm just sayin' without his help we might still be lookin' for D.B. Cooper."

"Uh, Paddy, people are still looking for D. B. Cooper."

"Sure, lad, you keep that myth alive." He leaned in even closer and whispered, "Two words. Condo. Burien." He leaned back and gave me a knowing wink. "Been sucklin' off the public teat for over forty-five years now, courtesy of yer own hallowed civil servants, but you didn't hear that from me, boyo. I run into him at the Bingo hall from time to time. A nice enough fella, but can't hear a lick no more. Ya has to shout everythin' his way. Goes by the name of Jonas Grumby."

"Jonas Grumby? That was the Skipper's name on Gilligan's Island."

"Was it now? Well, how do you like that. Clever lad."

Bastard had me going there. Dammit. There goes my Pulitzer.

"So back to the Swami. You're telling me—seriously—that he might have some insight into what's been going on around here?"

"That I am, boyo, that I am."

"But the guy's a two-bit con artist, taking grieving widow's checks to speak with their dear departed! He's nothing but a flim-flam man!"

"And what makes you the resident expert on the supernatural and hereafter?"

"I'm just saying that…"

Paddy cut me off in short order. "You're just sayin'. You're just sayin'! Well *I'm* just sayin' when you've been on the streets as long as Paddy Wagon you see a few things that don't have no rhyme nor reason, and you begin to question what's possible and what's not. So here's a nickel's worth of advice: Listen to what the man has to say. If you're not havin' what he's dishin' out, then you're none the worse for wear. But if me dear Swami is half the man I think he is, well, by gosh and begorrah, you may just find yourself one step closer to the promised land."

And with a saluting knuckle to the brim of his helmet, he was off to work the room, and I was left to struggle with the idea of calling on the Seattle Soothsayer to help me write a story.

The next day I found the Swami in his usual digs, camped out in the corner of the Pike Place Market Magic Shop, reading the palm of some sap tourist who was eagerly lapping up the local color. I caught the tail end of the exchange. The Swami's big, bellowing voice ricocheting around the cozy shop as he stared deeply in the woman's sweaty palm.

"Yes, yes, I see by your Sun line that great things are ahead of you. You see, the Sun line, also known as the Apollo line, is tremendously important."

The tourist was eating it up with a spoon. I did my best to keep my gag reflex in check. She leaned in earnestly. "Tell me, Swami, why is it called the Sun line?"

The Swami stroked his long white beard like he was deep in thought. He was probably turning over the betting line on the Seahawks game. "Well you see my dear, the name of the Sun line originates from the Mount of Moon, which is located on the base of the palm, little finger side, right here."

He delicately touched her palm, and I swear the woman shuddered. I threw up in my mouth.

"…and descends upward to the Mount of Sun, located below the ring finger which is also called the Apollo finger."

Another touch. Another shudder. Another taste of my breakfast.

The Swami readjusted his yellow turban and continued on. "As you can see here, as plain as the nose on my face, that your Sun line is spectacularly long. Why, I've not seen a Sun line as long as yours in many a moon."

Sun line. Many a moon. The man had no shame. He continued his spiel. "The Sun line mainly shows a person's capabilities, talent and popularity which may lead to success. The Sun line is also called the Line of Success."

The woman was practically falling out of her chair. "What? What do you see?"

The Swami's eyes bore deep into his mark's palm. "I see… I see… achievement! I see accomplishment. I see…"

He locked eyes with the swooning woman and gave her the full treatment. I had to admit, the guy knew how to work it.

"I see…unlimited potential."

It was like the guy was hocking Amway.

"Has any recognition recently come your way, my dear?"

The woman's eyes lit up like a roman candle. "I just got a promotion at the Sunglass Hut!"

The Swami threw out his arms like he'd just struck psychic gold. "The first of many, I foresee!"

The woman excitedly paid the Swami his $20 and raced off, probably to post her amazing supernatural experience on Facebook. The Swami coolly pocketed the bill and turned his gaze my way. He didn't break character and beckoned me to his table with a sweeping gesture of his fingerless gloved hands. "Come, join me for a look into your soul, my good man!"

I took a seat. "Trust me, you don't want to look inside my soul, Pastrami."

"Then what can I do for you? Wait..." He held his palm theatrically to his forehead. "You are on a mighty quest and seek answers from the Swami."

I locked him with deadpan eyes. "Wow. That must have been a tough one. I've got a better idea, tell me this week's Powerball numbers instead."

The Swami didn't bat an eye. I guess when you've been doing this charade as long as he has you've fine-tuned your knee-jerk reaction to hecklers and non-believers. He wagged a hand dismissively. "My powers are not for such tawdry means. Come. Sit. Let the Swami lessen the burden that you carry."

I rolled my eyes and leaned in on the faded, threadbare, velvet-covered card table. At one point, it may have been a deep burgundy, but now was nothing more than faded dusty rose. I said, "Look, if it were strictly up to me I wouldn't be here, but a friend of mine seems to think you might be of some assistance."

"Your friend, a certain Officer Paddy Wagon?"

I sat up. "How did you know that? Did Paddy call and let you know I was coming?"

The Swami's eyes twinkled with amusement. "He did not call. The Swami needs no calls to know why you are here."

"Okay, so I'll bite, why am I here?"

"You are perplexed by strange and puzzling ways that are spreading throughout our fine city. You come to the Swami with questions as to what, as you like to say, is up."

I was still convinced Paddy tipped him off, but I played along. "Bingo. So, tell me, oh Swami of Pastrami, what do you see in your crystal ball?"

"Funny you should ask," he said, and promptly pulled out a sparkly blue orb. But it sure weren't no crystal. Looked more like cheap rubber. Like it would be more at home in a game of kickball. I'm pretty sure I could see the inflation valve on the side. But whatever, the Swami held it aloft like it was the Holy Grail itself. "Behold, the eye of Ra! Where deep within its cosmic layers you may witness things that have been, and things that still may be." He paused for a dramatic moment and added, "And perhaps even what could have been."

This line caught my ear. "What do you mean, could have been?"

"Have you heard the term Alternate Universe?"

"Sure, I watched Star Trek. Why?"

He made a theatrical sweep of his arms and cast his eyes around the room. "This pale existence before you is merely one of many taking place at this very moment."

"What do you mean?"

"I mean this so-called reality that we traipse through is simply one version of countless others. Who's to say ours is the one true reality? There are quite possibly millions of other versions of this moment taking place in nearly identical circumstances, but the outcomes will all be different."

"Baloney!"

"It's Pastrami, but I digress. You only presume your reality is the only one because of your limited psychic vision."

"You got that right, pal. I don't have psychic vision, and dollars to donuts says you don't either."

The Swami sighed deeply and looked skyward, "You give them eyes, yet they do not see." He then turned back to me. "Would you like to visit one of these alternate universes?"

Now that was an offer I couldn't refuse. "Me? Visit an alternate universe? This I gotta see. What, you gonna hypnotize me? Slip me a mickey and plant subliminal suggestions in my head?"

The Swami didn't blink. "I offer you a rare glimpse into what our fair Seattle could have been."

"What do you mean, could have been?"

"Again, alternate universe. There are a multitude of versions of Seattle on a multitude of cosmic planes. This one you wake up to is the one you're familiar with because it is the only one you've known. Everything that it is is a direct result of a long line of decisions, actions and consequences."

"Okay, I follow. So what?"

"So suppose things went differently on numerous occasions throughout history. Do you think Seattle would be the same place it is now?"

"Probably not."

"Let me ask you something, Mr. Street, how do you perceive Seattle?"

"How do I perceive it?

"Yes, what is the consensus opinion of how people think of Seattle? What is its, shall we say, vibe?"

"That's easy. We're polite, tolerant, well-educated and a little full of ourselves at how good we've got it."

The Swami nodded, "A fair assessment. Now suppose things happened that changed the course of history. Suppose over a long period of time enough things changed that a completely different breed of individual decided to call the Pacific Northwest home. What do you think would happen?"

"Well, I suppose if the people were different the attitudes would be different."

"And when people and attitudes change, what else changes?"

I saw where he was going with this. "The vibe."

"Correct. An entire city's vibe can change when people's attitude's change. And as of this moment you feel the city's attitude is changing right before your eyes."

The old fool was actually making sense. I couldn't deny it. "Yeah, that's pretty much the shape of things."

The Swami held out his "crystal ball". "Would you like to now see what can happen when numerous actions change the course of a city's history? The consequences?"

How could I turn it down? "Okay, Swami. Let's see what you've got."

The Swami held the ball before my eyes and circled his magic wand above it. And by "magic wand" I mean a foot-long stick of half-inch doweling, painted black with a couple inches of white duct tape at the tips. The Swami conjured up his best stage voice. "Gaze deep into the Eye of Ra. Deep. Deeeeeep. Deeeeeeeeeeep."

Before I knew it, everything started getting blurry. The sounds of the magic shop vaporized and all I could hear was a sort of white noise. Eventually, sights and sounds began to re-crystalize. It was like I was watching TV. No, it was exactly like I was watching TV. As a matter of fact, I was watching channel 4, KOMO. It was the beginning of a newscast with two anchors I'd never seen before. Which was weird, because I knew the KOMO anchors, and the two I was watching on camera wasn't them.

"Good evening, I'm Bruce Sullivan…"

"And I'm Ginger Cameron. Development overkill. That's what some people are saying about the forest of construction cranes that fill the city skyline. Tonight, in a special report we'll be looking at civic and commercial construction projects throughout Seattle that are making headlines and give you some background on why many of them were so controversial in the first place."

A box graphic appeared over her shoulder depicting a silhouette of Seattle's skyline populated with numerous cranes. In block text below it, *Building Confidence?* Ginger pitched to the on-scene reporter. "We begin our live team coverage tonight with a report from Mercer Island."

The scene cut to a female reporter standing along a tree-lined waterfront. There were not homes or buildings of any kind in the background. The lower third name key labeled the reporter as Annette Grasso. I wasn't familiar with her. She began her report, all business.

"Yes, Ginger, we are here on Mercer Island where a local developer is, well, frankly, he's trying to fight city hall. Mr. Jonathan Yovin is seeking an exemption to the 1911 Bogue Plan that dictates that Mercer Island be restricted from development. Mr. Yovin is hoping to find a loophole in the 105-year-old plan in an effort to build a series of condominiums along the waterfront to cash in on the region's skyrocketing growth and land shortage. Virgil Bogue, the engineer who created the visionary Bogue Plan that completely reshaped the region, wrote in his original plan that the city was to, quote, "acquire Mercer Island and set aside these 4,000 acres as an island park—a people's playground, worthy of the city of millions which will someday surround Lake Washington." End quote. The plan has stood the test of time for over 100 years, but one local developer is hoping that time has passed. From Mercer Island, I'm Annette Grasso, KOMO 4 news."

The scene cut back to the male anchor, Bruce Sullivan, in the studio. "Thanks, Annette. The waterfront tunnel is Seattle's biggest construction project and hasn't been without its share of troubles, and naysayers. But proponents of the tunnel say they have a compelling reason why citizens should get on board with the project. We take you now live to the Lake Washington Tunnel where reporter Mike Sandoval is standing by."

Mike, another reporter I didn't recognize, was standing in front of a busy stream of traffic coming and going through a tunnel entrance I'd never seen before. He began his report.

"With all the fuss about the Viaduct coming down, proponents of the waterfront tunnel project have a simple, and powerful argument. And I'm standing beside it right now: The Lake Washington Tunnel. The waterfront tunnel group is saying the city made a tunnel from Seattle to Kirkland under Lake Washington and it's been working just fine for over 100 years. The tunnel, part of the earlier mentioned Bogue Plan, has had its share of problems over the years but by and large has been a stable and consistent route linking east and west-siders. And unlike the I-90 bridge that infamously sank in 1990 the Tunnel has not had any catastrophic accidents or structural failures. Ginger and Bruce?"

Back at the anchor desk, Ginger thanked the reporter and tossed to the next story.

"Another Bogue Plan project that was fought against is our own Civic Center, home to all the city's government buildings, where a massive retrofitting is going on right now. KOMO 4's Tess Henson is at city hall with this report. Tess?"

48

Tess was an attractive brunette with violet eyes to die for. She was standing in front of a line of buildings I'd never seen in my life. They looked like something out an Italian visitor's guide.

"Ginger, Seattle has long drawn sightseers to a most unusual location—our city hall. Well, technically the Civic Center that city hall is part of. Seattle proudly boasts the only government buildings in America that would look more at home in Europe. But sadly, these beautiful buildings have been falling into disrepair, and the concern for decades now has been that one sizable earthquake could bring them crumbling down. And that is why this retrofit is about to take place. For the next 12 months visitors will be greeted with a lot of scaffolding instead of the white marble they have become accustomed to.

"Some quick history about the Civic Center, the plan was greatly influenced by the City Beautiful movement of the early 1900s. Surrounding an oval-shaped plaza here at Fourth and Blanchard, the neo-classical courthouse, federal building, library, art museum and city hall—complete with 15-story tower—were designed with the Italian masters in mind. What's interesting is that the Civic Center almost never happened because downtown business owners didn't like the idea of moving the city's hub so far north. At the time the heart of downtown was Pioneer Square and the powerful businessmen at that time wanted to keep it that way. Luckily for us more progressive minds won out and for the decades since we have been able to enjoy this remarkable architectural achievement. And once the retrofit is complete we should be able to enjoy it for many more decades to come. From the steps of city hall, I'm Tess Henson, KOMO 4 news."

The newscast was baffling on so many levels. I didn't recognize the anchors or the reporters, and I knew every TV personality in this town. And the stories didn't make any sense. Mercer Island a park? A tunnel under Lake Washington? A European renaissance themed civic center? None of these things existed. I felt like I was in a Twilight Zone episode. The newscast continued. Bruce on set.

"A more recent civic project is in the news today. Well, recent compared to the Civic Center. We have an anniversary in South Lake Union. Tove Arnevik reports."

The scene changed to a shot of South Lake Union, at least I'm pretty sure it was South Lake Union. I could see the Lake in the background, but something about the surroundings didn't look quite right. In moments I knew why, as the perky reporter explained.

"An anniversary indeed, Bruce. If the South Lake Union Commons were human it would now be of legal drinking age. It's been 21 years since the city passed the property tax levy that funded the Commons—this gorgeous 61-acre park that has become Seattle's back yard; a green space right on the fringes of downtown Seattle, where people come to relax and play. Many still refer to it as Seattle's own version of New York's Central Park, and other than the size the similarities can't be ignored. Before the Commons, Seattle was one of the few large West Coast cities that didn't have a centralized gathering place. While San Francisco has Golden Gate Park and Vancouver has Stanley Park, Seattle was left wanting. For those too young to remember, the idea for the Commons was first proposed by Seattle architect Fred Bassetti and Seattle Times columnist John Hinterberger in 1991. This area used to be populated with about 130 small businesses and wasn't exactly one of the city's high-rent communities. But once the park was created the surrounding area suddenly became very attractive to burgeoning businesses like Amazon and the like. But as you can see behind me, there's no shortage of families here enjoying the sunshine and open spaces. Truly makes you appreciate the forward-thinking citizens from a generation ago who had the vision to see what a wonderful addition the Commons could make to Seattle."

Before the reporter even tossed back to the anchors I was well into a double-take. Wait, the Commons? That idea was shot down years ago! I

51

worked with John Hinterberger, and I remember how pissed he was when his idea fell through. Had to listen to him gripe for weeks. Now almost all of South Lake Union is Amazon central. This was getting weirder by the minute.

The scene cut back to the news studio where Ginger Cameron was introducing yet another puzzling story.

"One of our last stops on our tour of Seattle civic projects is one that was home to perhaps our city's most contentious political battle—the monorail. Or lack of monorail, as the case may be. For all the trouble the monorail conflict has caused over the years there are some positives that have come out of it. Tonight, we look at one of those success stories. We take you to Ballard where reporter Craig Pittman has a live report on the increasing popularity of the monorail green line."

The next shot was of the reporter standing by what was clearly a monorail station, but it was equally clear that it wasn't the Seattle Center line, Seattle's only monorail line. What gives? The reporter filled in the blanks.

"A new station has been added to the monorail green line that runs from Ballard to West Seattle. The 17-station line, which encountered fierce opposition when initially proposed, was completed in 2009. The green line was the first of what was supposed to be an X-shaped, five-line monorail system, but the other four lines never materialized due to financing issues. One of the arguments against the green line was that ridership would not be noticeably different from what the bus lines were already achieving. However, the riders we spoke to seem to feel that riding 30 feet above the streets was simply more enjoyable that riding in traffic at street level. I even heard a few people say that taking the monorail made the commute more fun, like a ride. In Ballard, I'm Craig Pittman for KOMO 4 News."

My head was spinning. But the next story completely knocked me off my feet. If I hadn't seen it I wouldn't have believed it. Bruce Sullivan set the stage.

"Seattle fans love their football, but our team could have had a very different history. KOMO sports director Richard Nye has a fascinating little-known story about not only the team's name but also where they play. Yep, another civic project that could have gone in a completely different direction. We take you now live to Elliott Bay Stadium. Richard?"

Wait, what? Elliott Bay Stadium? They had to be freakin' kidding me. They cutaway to a shot of the Sports Director standing by a large stadium entrance. But what threw me was that as he was doing his report he slowly walked away from the entrance, and you could see the wide expanse of Elliott Bay take over the background. If I'd had a paper bag I would have started breathing into it. I watched, lightheaded.

Richard began, "You can be sure the 12s will be out in force this Sunday as our Seattle Kings continue on their quest for a third Super Bowl appearance by taking on the San Francisco 49ers. The weather forecast calls for sunny skies so we can expect a whole flotilla of boats surrounding the dome—and the roof will be open. This is the type of weather that makes you really appreciate having the only floating stadium in the world. It's hard to imagine that the plan for the stadium here on Elliott Bay by West Harrison Street was almost scrapped in favor of building a cement, non-retractable domed stadium south of Pioneer Square. Can you imagine? A concrete domed stadium in that part of town? A little King's football trivia for you: Seattle had been trying to land a professional football team as early as 1958. In 1969, a group calling itself the "Seattle Sea Lions Management Corporation" was formed in an effort to secure a franchise. The potential team was renamed the Kings in 1971 for a couple of reasons. First, because the team would be playing in King County, and also because Washington Huskies football legend Hugh "The King" McElhenny was hired as Vice President and General Manager of the not-yet-existing team. So now you know.

"For the game on Sunday, it has just been announced that to raise the 12th Man flag on game day will be none other than "King" Felix Hernandez. How appropriate. Back to you in the studio."

They cut back to the news studio as Bruce and Ginger traded smiles and nodded approvingly. Bruce handled the wrap-up.

"Fascinating stuff, Richard. It's amazing to think about how different Seattle could have turned out if many of these projects and ideas never came to fruition. I guess we'll just have to consider ourselves lucky they went the way they did. Thanks for joining us tonight. We'll see you back here at 11 o'clock for a special report on Seattle's increasingly popular subway system and the controversial policies being enacted by the newly elected mayor of the city dump, Boris S. Wort."

The scene blurred again and I was instantly transported back into the magic shop. I tore my eyes away from the blue orb and looked around the room. Everything looked Jake; no one seemed to take notice of me and the Swami.

Speaking of the Swami, I turned to him, slightly more than a little pissed off. "What the hell was that? I look into your, whatever you call that thing, and the next thing I know I'm watching some wacky newscast. What gives?"

The Swami coolly replied. "Not what you were expecting?"

"I don't know what I was expecting, but, yeah, I guess a local newscast wasn't at the top of my list."

"And this newscast, was there anything… unusual about it?"

I told the Swami what I saw. About the different anchors and reporters. How the stories were about things in Seattle that didn't exist. At this last observation, the Swami smiled.

"They don't exist in *this* reality."

"But your point is…"

"Different decisions, different outcomes. Different outcomes…"

I finished his thought. "Whole different ballgame. Okay, fine, so you're showing me how Seattle could have been a totally different place if some decisions had been made differently. I get it. But what's going on around town right now isn't about decisions, it's about attitude. People are acting differently. They're not acting…Seattleish!"

"Ah, but different attitudes lead to different decisions."

The picture was still a little fuzzy but I was beginning to see an outline. What seemed to be coming into focus was a variation on a long con. A very long set of dominos that have to be painstakingly set up so when you tip over the first one, a whole chain of events kicks off that eventually leads to the last domino falling over.

"So you're saying this change in attitude I'm seeing around Seattle is part of some bigger game?"

The Swami slowly stroked his beard. "Perhaps."

I let that sink in a moment. "Then if that's the case that means the change in attitude has been manually created. That it's been orchestrated."

"That is a distinct possibility."

I shook my head at the thought. "But that's impossible! Nobody can change an entire city's behavior. And even if they could, why? What's the end game?"

The Swami seemed to smile at this revelation. "I see you have now found the deeper questions. Perhaps I can offer one last suggestion. MOHAI."

"MOHAI? The Museum of History and Industry? What can I find there?

"These alternate events you beheld within the Eye of Ra. Perhaps a bit of research on their history may provide some valuable insight."

Damn. He had me there. The difference between a hack writer and someone who actually knew what the hell they were talking about always came back to research. He who digs the deepest usually wins. I finally felt like I had a thread to hold onto. Now it was time to start the unraveling.

Like it or not, I had to accept the fact that this two-bit charlatan may have helped me get over the hump. I don't know how he did what he did, but all I know is my compass was finally pointing me in a direction I could follow. I tossed him twenty bucks and then threw in another finsky for good measure. A source is a source is a source. Maybe he wasn't such humbug after all.

Who am I kidding. His yellow turban was spray painted.

The Museum of History and Industry is easily Seattle's coolest museum. All things iconic-Seattle find a home inside their walls. Back in elementary school, it seemed we were always taking field trips there. One of my favorite exhibits was Bobo the gorilla. I freely admit that I'm old enough to remember seeing him alive. He died at the tender age of 17, in 1968. His bones went to the Burke Museum but the rest of him, stuffed and standing proudly, was now behind glass adorned with the clever line, *Gorilla in our Midst,* a play off the 1988 Sigourney Weaver - playing - naturalist - Dian Fossey - movie, Gorillas in the Mist. Back in the day, Bobo was a star at the Woodland Park Zoo, especially with kids. He was an even bigger star before that. He lived in the home of an Anacortes couple for the first two years of his life. I guess in 1951 you could get away with that kind of thing. The couple, Raymond and Jean Lowman, raised Bobo not so much as a pet, but almost more like a child. They dressed him in human clothes, taught him to eat at a table and sleep in a bed, and worked tirelessly to make him comfortable around other people. Needless to say, when word got out, the media ate it up; Bobo became a national celebrity. But gorillas are not naturally inclined to live in human homes and by 1953 the Lowman's realized the living situation was becoming untenable and turned Bobo over to the zoo. Over the next 15 years, Bobo was arguably Woodland Park's biggest attraction. In death, it's fair to say he's one of MOHAI's star attractions as well. But on this day, Bobo wasn't on my agenda.

The museum was originally located near Husky Stadium, tucked away on a side street where you needed a divining rod and bloodhound to find it. It now resided at a more user-friendly location on the shores of South Lake Union in the old armory building.

Upon entering MOHAI, I strolled into the expansive grand atrium and did a brief once-over of some of the first impression displays: The ancient U.S. Postal Service bi-wing seaplane hanging from the ceiling, the giant Rainier beer R at the south end of the room, and the always crowd-pleasing pink Lincoln Towing Toe-Truck, parked a few yards to the right.

A quick question to a helpful docent pointed me in the right direction—a display called "What if Seattle had built these projects?" Kismet. Up the stairs and around the bend, and just about everything I saw in the Swami's crystal ball was right there before me, and a few I hadn't seen as well: The failed Duwamish Valley monorail proposal of 1911—five decades before the Century

21 World's Fair Exposition that brought us our only existing monorail, the 1926 plan to replace the Pike Place Market with a massive building that ran from First Avenue down to the waterfront—40 years before the grass roots effort to save the market from demolition, the airport that was proposed for Madison Park, but, thankfully, voted down at the polls.

While wading through the assorted stories a familiar name cropped up. I was in the middle of the Bogue Plan history, reading about how powerful and influential businessmen dissuaded the public to vote for creation of the civic center at the proposed location at the north end of downtown. In 1910 Seattle's hub of business and political activity resided around Pioneer Square and these businessmen were not keen on the idea of city hall and company pulling up stakes and relocating, as mentioned in the Swami's newscast. One businessman, in particular, seemed to hold exceptionally strong sway over the others—a slick talking immigrant of questionable parentage, who made his fortune in businesses of equally questionable repute. A Mr. Morris S. Wort.

Hmmmm.

The driving force behind the push to tear down Pike Place Market? A wealthy widower who apparently had the goods on virtually every power broker in the region, and wasn't above the fine arts of blackmail and collusion. Her name? Doris S. Wort.

I was beginning to see a pattern.

It was no secret that the Wort family had a long and colorful history of being a collective thorn in the side of Seattle movers and shakers, and frequently traded favors with the upper crust to further their personal agendas, but what I was seeing here was far beyond anything I could imagine. These were concerted efforts that resulted in seismic shifts in Seattle's political, geographical and cultural landscape. These were efforts that changed Seattle's essence. The question, though, was did these efforts change things for the better or the worse. I suppose that's a subjective question, and other events that took place in the meantime could have affected that essence as well. There's no question they had an impact, and it was becoming abundantly clear that another branch on the Wort family tree was attempting to live up to his predecessors.

Boris S. Wort was trying to change Seattle's vibe.

So, there it was. I finally knew the who and the what. What I didn't know was the how or the why. I finished my ah-ha moment and headed for the exit. Along the way, I walked past fresh construction. The work area was a mess of saw horses, scattered tools, and sawdust. But it was the hole in the ground that grabbed my attention. A circular black hole, two feet across, with the tip of a ladder sticking up out of it. And up through that hole came the only person I know who travels by hole, none other than Leroy Frump, the unhandiest handyman you will ever find. His white tee shirt, floppy black hat, and suspenders were a dead giveaway. I had to get in a hello.

"Hey, Leroy! What's up?"

Leroy climbed up out of the hole and spun around clumsily before spotting me. "Heeeyyy, Mithter Street!"

Leroy's childlike innocence was his calling card. I don't think the man had a thought in his head or a mean bone in his body. And the man couldn't plane a door or plumb a sink to save his life, but for reasons I will never understand, he was always working. I know J.P. kept him busy down at the city dump, but still. The man was never at a loss for work.

Leroy always reminded me a bit of Red Skelton's character Clem Kadiddlehopper, with his infectious smile, puppy dog enthusiasm and slightly-lispy speech.

I walked up to Leroy and did what everyone did when they walked up to Leroy, I snapped his suspenders. He recoiled with an ouch, "Doggone it!" And before you knew it he was back to his old self, ready to help out. "Uh, what brings you here, Mithter Street?"

I always found it odd how he lisped on some words that had the letter S but not on others. "Research, Leroy, research."

"Workin' on another big article for the paper, are ya?"

"Maybe so, Leroy, maybe so." I always seemed to repeat myself with Leroy. Maybe because the man had the IQ of a dead light bulb. Leroy was dumb as a box of rocks but as I said earlier, everyone's a source. Who knows, maybe even Leroy had noticed a change in the air, but I wasn't banking on it. "So, Leroy, a question, have you noticed anything unusual lately?"

Leroy fixed me with a look as blank as a Kardashian's list of accomplishments. "Uh, whaddaya mean by unusual?"

"You know, anything out of the ordinary. People acting strangely?"

Leroy thought long and hard on the question. I thought he might hurt himself. Finally, "As a matter of fact I have."

This surprised me. I didn't really expect to get anything out of Leroy. I couldn't wait to hear what he considered unusual.

"Well, thir, just a few days ago I was walkin' down California Avenue—you know where California Avenue is, Mithter Street?"

I nodded impatiently. "Yes, Leroy, main drag in West Seattle. Lots of shops and restaurants. Tough to miss."

Leroy just smiled the smile of a child. "Yeth it is. Well thir, I was walkin' along, headin' to another job, when I notithed something kinda strange."

"In what way?"

"Well, thir, the people walkin' the other way on the sidewalk looked me square in the eye. Ever last one of them."

"Wait, you're saying everyone made eye contact with you…and held it?"

Leroy nodded like an Edgar Martinez bobblehead. "Yeth thir, they did."

Leroy wasn't kidding. That was damn peculiar. People in Seattle were practically allergic to eye contact. They glance, give a quick tight-lipped smile and then promptly turn their attention to the pavement. It's all part of the Seattle Freeze.

Leroy seemed to brighten up at my reaction. "Did I help ya, Mithter Street? Huh, did I?"

"You may have, Leroy, you may have." I almost felt like I should pat him on the head or scratch him behind the ears. "Well, gotta go, Leroy. Keep up the good work."

As I was walking away Leroy yelled out to me, "Anytime you need any more help, Mithter Street, I'm right here for ya. Anytime at all."

My trip to MOHAI had paid dividends, but I still had a lot of wood to chop. I strolled along the path that bordered the south end of Lake Union and watched a Kenmore Air seaplane as it was just coming in for a landing. As long as I can remember I always got a kick out of watching those seaplanes take off and land and would usually stop what I was doing to watch it happen. It was early October; we were on the tail end of a classic Seattle Indian summer. September was amazing and the first stages of October were following suit. There was a bite in the air offering a hint of temperatures to come, but for the time being, it was still damn pleasant. I pulled up a seat on one of the benches and enjoyed a few moments of people watching. The vast majority were probably Amazonians on their lunch breaks, but I caught more than a fair share of stay at home moms out for a run or taking their kids to the museum. Seattle fashion was out in all its casual glory. Lots of jeans, tee shirts or Seahawks jerseys for the guys and a healthy dose of sweaters or Seahawk jerseys and…wait for it…yoga pants for the women—probably those cheapies I saw advertised on TV. A couple walked by and I could smell Seattle's ubiquitous fall aroma: pumpkin spice. Latte's, of course. As a game, I started a count. Over the course of 30 minutes I counted 73 people carrying Starbucks coffee cups—mostly Grandes—and virtually every one of them within sniffing distance left a vapor trail of pumpkin spice in their wake.

I hung out on the bench for quite a while, turning over the facts in my head. I knew I had a blockbuster story on my hands if I could only piece the whole thing together.

The old axiom in the newsroom is "If it bleeds, it leads", meaning that violent or catastrophic events frequently begin your newscast. What was going on right now was certainly not violent. Was it catastrophic? As of now, no. But all my reporter instincts told me that the go-cart was just beginning to roll down the hill, and according to gravity, would only build up speed until it reached terminal velocity. By that time, it would be too late to throw on the brakes, and in the end, you're being cleaned off the pavement with a hook scrape and a sponge. I was getting the distinct feeling it's like the old frog in a pot of water thing. Drop him in boiling water and he'll hop out instantly. Put him in cold water and turn the heat up slowly and Mr. Frog doesn't notice the lethal temperature climb until it's too late. If Boris was indeed behind whatever was going on he was taking a completely new tack for him. Usually Boris likes to make a splash. You know, try to knock over the Space Needle, sink a ferry or blow up the Ballard Bridge. Run of the mill villain stuff. But a slowly developing, long drawn out plan would be a complete paradigm shift for Wort. Frankly, the prospect was more than concerning. It was like a slow fuse had been lit, and eventually, there was going to be an explosion. That's why what had been going on hadn't hit the newscasts yet. The explosion hadn't gone off yet. Nothing had been bleeding.

I decided I needed to do a little Wort research before going any further so I beat cheeks to Wallingford and the Seattle Meowtropolitan, Seattle's first, and only cat cafe. Astrid can only go a couple of days before she needs a kitty fix, and there's no better place than this cat-friendly coffee house. Astrid likes coffee and tea as much as any Seattleite, but she's sort of the odd duck in that you'll never catch her in a Starbucks. She's of the mind that there are plenty of mom and pop coffee shops that need her business more than the SoDo Siren. That and the fact that she's not the biggest Howard Schultz fan, after that stunt he pulled with the Sonics and the boys from Oklahoma City.

I found Astrid absentmindedly sipping a chai tea while trying to capture the attention of orange striped tabby on the other side of a large window. The café is separated into two parts: the regular café and the cat lounge. You can book a reservation to mingle with the cats in the cat lounge, or you can hang out on the other side of the glass and be content with simply watching them. The cat lounge is a big, open space with assorted platforms and ramps built around a couple of the main support pillars in the center of the room.

There are six resident cats who call the café home, but the rest of the other dozen or so felines that hang out there are all up for adoption. I have to say, management runs a pretty tight ship. You can't just walk in and adopt up a cat on a whim, you have to fill out an adoption application, and then you're entered in the queue. It's sort of like PAWS or the Humane Society, but with more comfortable chairs and biscotti.

I stood behind Astrid for a good minute before her spidey senses told her I was there. She continued waving to the cat and sipping her tea, not bothering to go to the trouble of giving her boyfriend eye-contact. "'Sup Street?"

I squatted down next to her and watched the tabby she was focused on not give her the time of day. While keeping my eyes on the cat I said in a half whisper, "What do you call a pile of kittens? A meowntain." Nothing. Not like I was expecting a response. I hit her with another. "Did you hear about the cat who ate a ball of yarn? She had a litter of mittens." Astrid didn't say anything but I think I got a tiny eye-roll out of her, which ain't bad, compared to what I usually got. It was our own little game when we would meet up at the cat café. I would tell bad cat jokes and she would ignore them. Although I suspect she would be heartbroken if I stopped the tradition.

She eventually turned my way. "What's on your mind?"

"I will tell you the moment I have a good mug of hot chocolate in my hands. Back in a flash." I walked up and placed my order and moments later I was back at Astrid's side, steaming cocoa in hand. The tabby was still ignoring her. I took a heat taste on the cocoa. It passed muster so I took another hit. Delish. I'm one of the local weirdos in that I'm a Seattleite who doesn't drink coffee. Go figure. I love coffee houses, love the atmosphere and love the smell, but the taste? Yuck. I remember back in my 20s I was on a date with my then girlfriend, an auburn beauty who eventually turned out to be a psycho of biblical proportions. We were at the movies. While making a popcorn run she asked me to grab her an espresso. I'd never tasted espresso, let alone ordered one so when the barista set out a Dixie-cup, half filled with a liquid as black as my first editor's soul, I actually did a double take. I stared at the cup, then back at the barista, then back at the cup. I finally asked, "Where's the rest?" She said, "Uh, that's it." I was more than slightly astonished. "That's it? Three bucks for that thimble?" Remember, I was new to this whole coffee/espresso thing. The line behind me was lengthening and the natives were getting restless so I finally shrugged it off and took the Dixie-cup back to my eagerly awaiting girlfriend. She took the tiny cup in both hands and took a long orgasmic sniff. I believe the woman actually shuddered. She took a sip and, as God as my witness, she groaned. We'd been dating for three months and I had yet to make her shudder, or groan for that matter. Hmm, on hindsight, maybe she broke up with me.

After watching this spectacle play out I finally had to see what all the fuss was about. "Can I have a sip?"

She was thrilled that I was interested. "Absolutely!"

I took the tiny cup and placed it to my lips. And my face instantaneously folded in on itself. "Good lord! You actually drink this stuff?"

"You don't like it?"

"Are you kidding me? I've never tasted anything so bitter in my life! I feel like Mike Tyson just punched me in the face! You actually go out of your way to drink this stuff? On purpose?"

Thus, my first experience with the strange world of coffee. Granted, this was espresso, not coffee, but the bean and I never did hit it off, which was fine by me.

Astrid was still patiently waiting for me to break my chocolate reverie. I said, "Has Wort been in the news lately? Maybe something below the radar that I haven't noticed?"

She thought on that for a second. "Nope. Nothing I can recall lately."

"Nothing?"

Astrid chewed her lip and shook her head. "Can't think of anything. Matter of fact, I think the last time he made an appearance was about six months ago. He was spotted in very un-Boris-like locations, rural areas. Didn't give it much thought at the time."

"Doesn't that strike you as a bit odd? Boris being so quiet for so long?"

"Now that you mention it, yeah, it does. Why the interest?"

I watched the tabby yawn and stretch. Probably the most energy he'd exerted in the last 12 hours. "It appears he may be somehow involved in the strange behavior I've been seeing around town.

"So what are you going to do, Sherlock?"

"Dunno. I'm still in research mode. Tell you what, tomorrow, do me a solid and quietly check with the assignment desk. See if any tips may have come in about Boris that didn't pan out. I'll go through the archives to see when was the last time he made print. It's damn peculiar that he's gone radio silent for this long. The man lives for the spotlight."

Everyone in the Puget Sound area was familiar with Wort. He's tough to miss, with the black cape, handle-bar mustache and off-kilter sneer. And that hat! Dusty, black felt. Peaked like Devil's Tower in Close Encounters, but without the top chopped. The front of the hat looks like the saggy brim had been snipped off with dull scissors and now hung down in front, held in place by three safety pins. The final touch: Two downward sloping, angry-shaped eye holes cut into the hanging cowl felt, giving Boris a look of perpetual up-to-no-good-ness. When he speaks, he sounds like an over-caffeinated Bela Lugosi—kind of a cartoon Hungarian accent. And he makes this crazy sound whenever he shows up. I'm not even sure how to describe it, let alone write it. It's kind of like he's rolling his tongue very quickly, very loosely. Sort of a bleh-dl-edl-edl-edl-edl sounding thing. Sort of.

Boris's claim to fame, which he is always more than happy to tell you, is that he's the second meanest man in the world. Not the fourth, not the third, but the second. Last I checked, the third meanest man in the world was some formerly low-rent villain out of Kenosha, Wisconsin who climbed in the rankings after pulling off an impressive stunt of evilness when he hacked the Fox television news network with 24 straight hours of Joanie Loves Chachi reruns. Frankly, I'm still not sure how the hack was any more evil than their regular line up, but whatever.

Boris has been hanging around as number two evil for some time now so it wouldn't surprise me if he finally had his sights set on the top dog. To be the first meanest man in the world is no small feat.

It takes patience and serious dedication to one's craft to reach the top spot. And a true understanding of evilocity. I know that's probably not a real word, but it ought to be. The current number one is a shadowy corporate figure in the McDonald's fast food organization who constantly dreams up new, barely edible Mc-something-or-others. He took over the top spot when he unleashed the McRib on the unsuspecting world population. He has yet to be, nor shall he ever be, forgiven.

Needless to say, it would take a devastatingly huge bit of evilness to knock him off the throne. But if anyone is up to the task, it would be Boris. I had the pleasure of doing a sit-down interview with him years back, right after he was officially labeled second meanest man in the world. It was a 3000-word feature piece in the PI's Sunday Arts and Entertainment section. I was initially struck by the man's laser focus and determination to cause mischief. It seemed like a week didn't go by when he wasn't trying to blow up the Ballard Locks or steal Ivar's secret recipe. What also stuck with me was his professionalism. He took his role as a purveyor of evil very seriously and worked tirelessly at trying to hone his nefarious skills. He spoke extensively about his daily regimen and how he always took a few moments each morning to focus on his breathing and center himself (Good air out, bad air in. Repeat 3 times.) He had, dare I say, a charming demeanor about him. A far cry from the dastardly Snidely Whiplash-type figure we've come to see on the nightly news. Throughout the interview he sat, one leg casually thrown across the other, his Chuck Taylor sneakers bouncing thoughtfully, as he regaled me with daring feats of naughtiness: how he secretly masterminded the move of the Seattle Pilots to Milwaukie after their inaugural season; his cooking of the city's books to quash the monorail plans, the monkey wrench he threw into Big Bertha's drive shaft to hold up the waterfront tunnel's progress for a year. The list goes on and on. Years later I heard that he took particular glee, and immense pride in allegedly tapping into Seahawks quarterback Russell Wilson's helmet speaker, and in his best Pete Carroll imitation, convinced him to throw a pass on second and goal on the one-yard line in Super Bowl XLIX. If true, why Boris didn't take the top spot after that I'll never know.

The one thing that put a crack in Boris's smooth demeanor when I was interviewing him, though, was when I brought up his arch nemesis, Julius Pierpont Patches, the Clown. No sooner did I mention him when Boris promptly stood and stormed out of the room, a look of clear annoyance writ large across his face, at least from what I could see of it from under his cowl. No spoilers here, but he and Patches have a past and at that time feelings were still pretty raw.

My phone rang, the screen said it was Astrid. I punched the button. "You got something?"

"Yes and no."

"Can you be more specific?"

"Yes, I got something, no it's not about Boris."

I waited. I know it must have been something pretty good because she was clearly enjoying dangling it in front of me. I took a page from her book and patiently waited her out, even though it was killing me, which she knew.

She finally coughed it up. "Who, other than Boris is Seattle's biggest troublemaker?"

"Could it possibly be a certain witch?"

Astrid gave an appreciative-sounding grunt. "I'm impressed. My source at the cop shop tells me Zenobia (gasp) has resurfaced more than a few times over the last year. Oddly enough, she made several appearances about six months ago and then completely vanished off the radar. Now, all of a sudden, she pops back up again just a couple of weeks ago? Seems a bit strange."

"I got similar intel. Gertrude spotted her at Uwajimaya not too long ago, stocking up on who knows what."

"Uwajimaya? Gertrude taking a Szechuan cooking class?"

"Beats me."

Astrid said, "That can't be good. Last time Zenobia (gasp) surfaced for any extended period of time you know what happened."

"You know they couldn't prove anything."

The event in question was back in early 1980. Zenobia (gasp) was popping up all over the place, particularly south of Mount Rainier. Suddenly she'd become a regular visitor in places like Winlock (Home of the world's largest egg!), Vader and Mossyrock. Hardly her normal stomping grounds. Word was that she was even getting cozy with a certain Mr. Harry Truman, of Mount St. Helens fame. Well, you don't need the Amazing Kreskin to devine what happened next. Zenobia (gasp) was allegedly spotted by a couple down by the Toutle River on the evening of May 17th. They said they were on a hike, off the normal trails—against all warnings, mind you, based on the mountain's recent rumbling activity—when they heard something that seemed a bit out of the ordinary: chanting. They claim they peered through a gap in some trees and saw what appeared to them to be an old woman dressed in flowing black robes and a pointed hat, reciting incantations from a large book, in between drawing obscure shapes in the air with her hands. They say they watched for a few minutes before moving along on their hike, writing it off as some weird tree-hugger thing. The hikers had been on a six-hour binge of Slim Jims and Clif Bars so rational thought was clearly beyond their reach, but still, what happened a mere 15 hours later made them think twice about what they purportedly witnessed. The following morning, at 8:32 Pacific Standard Time, Mount St. Helens went seismic, half the mountain vanished, Toutle Lake vanished, Harry Truman vanished and the entire world turned their eyes to the suddenly newsworthy Pacific Northwest.

Did Zenobia (gasp) cause the eruption? No one can say. There was an investigation, oaths were sworn, interviews given and reports taken, but nothing came of it. It was chalked up to, as they say in insurance parlance, an act of God. The couple who claim they saw Zenobia (gasp) that day were from Eugene, Oregon, so their testimony was seen as questionable at best.

If the witch was indeed responsible for the St. Helens eruption that would have easily catapulted her into the upper rankings of evilness. Could she have achieved First meanest *woman* in the world stature? Perhaps. But for some odd reason, Zenobia (gasp) never went out of her way to grab headlines. Unlike Boris S. Wort, she seemed content to cause catastrophe, or at the very least, disruption, and then vanish into the woodwork without any regard for the resulting media firestorm.

I guess that shouldn't really come as a surprise, considering her roots. Born and raised on the

Washington coast in hardscrabble Aberdeen, back when the mills were still hiring and the local economy hadn't gone in the tank, she grew up in a conservative family and largely kept to herself. Studious and hard-working were frequently used descriptives for the young not-yet-witch. That, and a reputation for bad luck. She made headlines in the local paper, The Daily World, on more than one occasion for her tough breaks. One such occurrence simply referred to as The Pigeon Incident, happened while she was out riding her Vespa through picturesque Sam Benn Park when she was struck in the face by a low flying pigeon. The impact of the instantly dead bird knocked the teenager unconscious. With Zenobia (gasp) slumped over and blissfully unaware, the scooter throttled up before clipping a cedar tree and pitching her onto the road, where she was then run over by a street-sweeper, breaking her leg in three places and giving her a world-class case of road rash. As a senior at Weatherwax High School she was voted Most Likely to win the lottery and lose the ticket. This may be the reason behind her lack of interest in the spotlight.

As a student Zenobia (gasp) seemed to have a preternatural knack for all things science and nature. Her teachers were convinced she had a promising future in Microbiology, but she began losing interest in traditional education models and soon dropped out of Grays Harbor Community College before her junior year. At this point she began showing an interest in the pagan ways. She was highly recruited by the local Wiccan community, but opted to stick to the fringes and freelance. At what point she crossed over to the dark side is anyone's guess. For all her run-ins with law enforcement over the years she still would surprise people with her causes and crusades. No one was ever willing to come out and say magic was behind it, but there was no denying the strange coincidence of how the small-town witch became enamored with an unheralded Aberdeen hard rock trio and evangelized for them at every turn. Soon after Nirvana became the hottest band on the planet.

When Zenobia (gasp) made the move to the big city issues began to arise in short order. Witchcraft was never at the forefront of Seattle politics, but it didn't take long before City Council members began pushing for more stringent oversight. After a string of inexplicable and catastrophic decisions—KIRO News goes "Outside-the-Box", Husky helmets are changed to purple, the Mariners trade Derek Lowe and Jason Varitek for Heathcliff Slocumb—local politicos weren't taking any chances, and promptly slapped heavy regulation on all things magic. Not that this was a huge deterrent for Zenobia (gasp). After all, it's tough proving in a court of law that sorcery is at work.

I thought for a moment. "So, we know Zenobia (gasp) was busy six months ago, then vanished and recently just as suddenly reappeared. Does that about cover it?"

"Yep. And we've also determined that Boris has been off the grid for approximately the same amount of time. Don't look now but it looks like our two troublemakers may be working in cahoots."

Nobody likes troublemakers working in cahoots.

I hung up the phone just in time to get a text message from Charlie Can Do. Charlie's not big on technology so it always surprises me when I get anything from him in electronic form. In typical Can Do style it was short and strange: *Search out the worm.*

I know of only one worm he could be talking about: Sturdly.

Seattle is an incredibly literate city. Number two in the country, behind Washington DC, last I checked. There are more bookstores than most other cities of equal size, and Seattle's 27 libraries are also used more frequently than the vast majority of the other cosmopolitan hubs of America, so it's no surprise that even the worms are well-read. Sturdly is considered the authority on all things book-related in our city. Literature professors from all over the world seek him out for advice and counsel. People still talk in reverent tones of his 1978 Harvard commencement speech. Legend has it Hemmingway himself made it a point to share a bottle with the worm whenever he was in town. Tequila, naturally. No word on whether any of Sturdly's relatives were in the bottle.

Sturdly makes his home in J.P.'s bookshelf but he spends a good deal of his waking hours at

Seattle's main library. It's not often that a city's library becomes a tourist attraction, but with the main branch's eye-catching architecture, it's become a designated photo op. All jutting angles and crisscrossing glass and steel, it's a cubist's fever dream of a library. The interior is a vast open space, flooded with natural light that beckons all readers. Upon arrival I wound my way to Sturdly's section of choice: History, and found him devouring a large tome on Indian tribes of the Pacific Northwest. And when I say devouring I actually mean devouring. As in eating. Shredding. Making mincemeat of binding, cover and page. The library is well aware of Sturdly's unusual eating habits and provides him a steady diet of well-worn copies of books that would otherwise be headed for the recycle bin. He came up for air long enough for me to get in a greeting.

"Hey, Sturdly. Tasty book you got there?"

He let out a surprisingly loud burp (for a worm, or in a library, for that matter) and nodded at me in acknowledgment. Sturdly's larger than your average night crawler. I'd put him at a good foot in length and about five inches wide; he's vibrant green, has bright, intelligent eyes and a little yellow tuft of hair sprouting from the top of his head. But probably his most distinguishing characteristic is his shirt collar—minus the shirt. He choked down a few more pages before greeting me. "Stewart Street, good of you to visit." He always sounds like he has a bad cold; completely stuffed up.

I cut to the chase. "I got a message from Charlie Can Do that you have something for me."

Sturdly flipped and flopped, as he frequently does. "I do, I do. I understand you're on the hunt for all things Wort."

"Correct. What can you tell me?"

"How much do you know about him?"

"About Boris? More than most, less than some."

Sturdly flopped around some more. "So, you know about his all-consuming desire to become the first meanest man in the world."

I rolled my eyes. "Every kid in the city knows that."

Sturdly gave me a knowing look. "Yes, but did you know *why* he's so determined to achieve that title?"

"Because he's an overachiever?"

Sturdly indicated toward a large hopper filled with distressed books. "For the price of several of those books I will tell you a story."

I fished out an armful and dumped them in front of the worm. They didn't last long. A buzz saw and shredder couldn't have made shorter work of them. Within moments he was ready to share his information.

"Boris S. Wort…" he paused. "Do you know what the S stands for?"

"Sacajawea? No idea."

"Same thing the S stands for in former President Harry S. Truman's name. Nothing. So, moving along…Boris lost his dad when he was too young to remember him, so he was raised solely by his mother, Doris."

"Yea, I read a little something about her. She sounded like a real piece of work."

"That she was. When her husband died, he left her with nothing but a baby boy and a stack of bills. You remember that scene in Gone with the Wind, right before intermission?

"Scarlet O'Hara, beaten down, making a pledge to the universe that she would rise from the ashes. Something about 'As God as my witness…' yadda, yadda, yadda. Sure."

Sturdly synopsized the rest of Scarlet's monologue. "You won't keep me down. I will do what I have to, even if I have to cheat, steal or kill."

"That was mama Wort's credo, huh?"

"Pretty much. And it worked. Nothing got in that woman's way, and young Boris got a front row seat through all of it." Sturdly paused long enough to chow down on another book—a treatise on swift decisions made by the Seattle City Council; more a pamphlet, really—before continuing with his story. "Boris was an only child, and as such, was a momma's boy. Spoiled rotten. Got whatever he wanted. He wasn't terribly popular, or much of a

88

student for that matter. As a result, he was an outsider, and typical of outsiders, he was picked on. A week didn't go by when Boris wasn't in the middle of a fight. But that was one thing Boris excelled at, the sweet science."

"Boris the brawler, huh?"

"When necessary. The man had a tremendous right hand and a granite jaw. But interestingly he was more of a technician, and became quite the boxing aficionado. He studied the art, not so much of hitting, but of not being hit. He spent hours in the gym. Apparently, his footwork was exceptional. His jump rope routine was legendary in the local boxing community. The man actually had his sights set on the U.S. Olympic team."

"Obviously, he didn't make it."

"No, and one can't help but wonder what might have been if he had. How his story arc would have changed if he became a world class boxer."

"What happened?"

"He was in training, just a young man, jogging through the University district—Greek Row—when he was heckled by some fraternity boys out on their front porch. Evidently it didn't sit well with young Wort. Are you familiar with the term 'roid rage? It's a real thing, and back in those days steroid use was de rigueur as part of a boxing training program."

"So he went and mixed it up with the frat boys?"

"More like cleaned their clocks. Thoroughly. Then went inside and, uh, relieved himself in the middle of their living room."

"Hoo, boy."

"He watched the Olympics from a jail cell."

"Wait, he went to jail for getting in a fight?"

"It wasn't his first."

"Ah."

"He'd already become a familiar houseguest of Seattle's finest. When he wasn't running afoul of the law he was traveling the world taking in all the major bouts: The Thrilla in Manila, Rumble in the Jungle, Hagler/Hearns, the Duran/Leonard No Mas fight, Tyson/Douglas, you name it, he was there. The fighting world was his passion. Go back and watch footage of any of the big fights, chances are you'll see him ringside. He developed a close relationship with Don King. I suspect it helped shape his yearning for the spotlight. It was also during this time that he began honing his evil skills, and he found the perfect foil for his escapades."

"J.P Patches."

"Precisely. No dummy, Wort, he saw the huge popularity of the Clown and his show, and realized that every hero needs a villain, and as Alfred Hitchcock said, your movie is only as good as your bad guy, or something like that. And to top it off, that accent of his?"

"Yea?"

"Totally affected."

"You're kidding."

"Nope. He felt it made him sound more menacing."

"So he's not from some Eastern Bloc country?"

"Try Mercer Island."

"Unbelievable."

"Say what you will about Boris, but he's a marketing genius."

I let this all settle into my brain and started connecting the dots. "He becomes a pest to J.P., starts getting face time, suddenly he becomes a household name."

"Correct. A masterful plan. Before long he's become a bit of a cult hero, even spawns a following."

"Boris Buddies."

"They had their own tee shirts and everything. The perfect antonym to Patches Pals."

"And for the next couple of decades he spends his time trying to mastermind plots to kidnap Esmerelda, disrupt Christmas or take over the show."

Sturdly nodded. "That last one seemed to be his primary focus. He was obsessed with taking over J.P.'s show. It became his white whale."

"And when the show went off the air?"

"Boris still needled the Clown when he could, but without the dangling carrot of the show he turned his attention to more civic disruption."

I nodded. "I think I've lost track of all the times he's threatened to blow up the Space Needle."

"The man is evil, but apparently plan execution is not his strong suit."

"That may have changed. I have reason to think Boris is behind a deeply involved plan to dramatically change Seattle's vibe, and that he's been plotting and slowly executing his master plan over an extended period of time."

"That would be very un-Boris-like."

"I know, right? But that's what the tea leaves are indicating right now."

I pitched Sturdly a few more books from the hopper and he quickly devoured them. After he finished I filled him in on my observations and suspicions. He listened thoughtfully and said, "That might explain this next piece of information." At which point he brought out an exquisitely handwritten note. The penmanship was flawless.

"What is it?" I asked.

"This I found sitting on my bookshelf back at the city dump. I then received a message from our mutual friend Charlie Can Do that it might be of value to you." He slid the note across the table with his nose. In perfect cursive, it read, *They specialize in this at Armstrong's aqua stop which will take you to the low-brow man of iron will.*

I looked up expectantly at Sturdly. "What the hell?" He gave the closest thing he could to a shrug.

"A clue. Evidently someone with information is in your corner and wants to help."

"So why not just come see me and tell me what they know?"

Sturdly gave another worm shrug. "Beats me."

I puzzled this over for a moment. "And how did Charlie know you would have this note and that it was for me? He's got to be involved somehow, right?"

"Who's the say with the Zen master. I gave up trying to figure that guy out a long time ago."

The clue didn't mean a thing to me, but I always had my go-to source for things like this. Astrid was the kind of person who did the New York Times crossword puzzle in pen. A puzzle like this was catnip to her. I shot her a text and she told me to meet her after work at Ray's Boathouse in Ballard. What better way to decipher clues than over an Old Fashioned during happy hour?

I found her at a window seat drinking in the unparalleled view of Shilshole Bay and the Olympic mountains. There aren't many restaurants in Seattle with better locations than Rays. The place was opened as a coffee house in 1945 by boat rental and bait house operator Ray Lichtenberger. He built the now-famous vertical sign that flashes RAY'S in bold red neon in 1952. Over the decades Ray's became synonymous with fresh seafood. In fact, Ray's was the first local restaurant to buy directly from fishermen. In 1987, at arguably its peak in popularity, it made news of the wrong sort when the boathouse burned down to its pier pilings. It was rebuilt, only to endure another, albeit smaller fire, practically ten years to the day later. Astrid does have a thing for iconic Seattle restaurants and drinkeries. Another reason why I dig her.

She was halfway through her cocktail, fishing the cherry out of the bottom of the tumbler—she never could wait before attacking the cherry, the one piece of impatience she seems to show. As per usual, without even glancing up at me... "'Sup, Street?"

I pulled up a chair and flagged down a waitress, ordered a seven and seven (or a 14 as I like to cleverly call them) and placed the note gingerly on the table. Astrid's eyes actually lit up a smidge. At least as much as a Norwegian is willing to allow. She slowly rotated the note around on the table and studied it carefully.

"Nice penmanship."

"I know, right?"

She read the clue aloud and propped her chin on her hand and chewed her lip. She sat like this for several minutes and I knew better than to interrupt her. When she's in full-blown problem-solving mode all external influences cease to exist. It's one of the reasons she's such a good reporter. After a while, her eyes still locked on the note, "That's a beauty all right."

"Nothing ringing a bell? No ideas?"

She glanced up at me with no small amount of disdain. "I didn't say that; I'm just acknowledging good work."

I took a hit of my 14 and crunched some ice. "So, what do you see?"

She tapped on the note. "To decode a puzzle like this you have to break it down into its base elements. Read it to me."

I rotated the note back around to face me and read it aloud. "They specialize in this at Armstrong's aqua stop which will take you to the low-brow man of iron will."

Astrid reached into her purse and pulled out her reporter's notepad and a pen. "Let's start with the who." She wrote out the clue and then underlined the word *they*. "At this point we don't know who *they* are."

"Boris and Zenobia (gasp), I presume, right?"

"Maybe, but my gut tells me it's not them. The *they* in this clue is tied to the next part of the clue, the *where*—Armstrong's aqua stop."

"What's Armstrong's aqua stop?"

"Don't know yet. But what we do know is that what they specialize in there will lead us to the second part of the clue, which is the low-brow man of iron will."

I felt like I was watching Abby Sciuto, the forensics expert on the CBS TV show NCIS, taking blood samples and bullet casings and figuring out who the murderer is. Astrid continued with her train of thought. "This is a procedural clue."

"Which means…"

"It means that we have to figure it out in steps. Solve the first part, which will lead us to the second part. So, let's begin with the where: Armstrong's aqua stop. First let's break this down into its own components: Armstrong. Aqua stop. We begin with Armstrong. Is Armstrong a person, place or thing?"

"I'm guessing a person."

"I'm guessing that too. Although in this context it could be a place or thing relating to a person."

My brain was already starting to hurt. "Okay, so let's say Armstrong is a person. Who's named Armstrong?"

Astrid didn't even blink. "Off the top of my head, I can think of two: Stretch Armstrong and Neil Armstrong."

Stretch Armstrong was the 1970s toy in the shape of a shirtless muscular man whose arms and legs could be stretched out a good foot in either direction. It was a terrific test of strength for pre-pubescent kids. The other Armstrong was Neil the astronaut, he of the "One small step for man, one giant leap for mankind." The first man on the moon.

Astrid kept rolling. "I have to believe it's one of those two. The clue wasn't given to completely stump you, it was given to help you out."

"So why didn't they just tell me where to go? Or better yet, forget this charade and just tell me what they know?"

Astrid smiled at this. "Because they don't want it to be too easy. Whoever this person is they're very smart, and have a sense of…"

"Humor?"

"I was going to say adventure. They're making it a game. Get the clues, figure out the clues, follow the trail, and bingo, you have your final answer. Frankly, I think this is pretty cool."

"Glad you're enjoying yourself. Personally, I'd rather not work this hard for my dinner, I'd rather it was simply served without the floor show."

Astrid sat back in her chair. "So, you'd rather have Daniel's Broiler over Teatro ZinZanni?"

"I'm a simple man of simple tastes. Just give me my steak and I'm happy. Song and dance not necessary."

"Where's the fun in that? A little song and dance, occasionally, can be fun. You've got a terrific story here and now the story just got more interesting."

"Okay, okay, you've made your case. Let's get back to the clue. Which Armstrong is it?"

She crossed her arms and gave me a look. "No. If you're going to be a weeny, I'm not going to do all your homework for you. I want to see if you can do a little detective work."

It was my turn to be petulant now. "Fine." I took another hit of 14 and looked at the note. After a moment, I looked out the window and watched a sailboat slowly cruise in towards the marina, obeying the 5-knot speed limit. My eyes drifted up to the sky. It was a partly cloudy evening edging into the golden hour, that small window of time after sunset but before it gets dark, when everything looks, well, golden. Folks in the film and video world also refer to it as the Magic Hour, because the lighting is so beautiful.

Peeking out from behind a cloud a crescent moon appeared. I turned back to Astrid. "I'm thinking it refers to Neil Armstrong."

"Why?"

"Because Stretch Armstrong is a bit too obscure. Like you said, whoever left the note wants it to be challenging but not impossible. Not everyone's going to know who Stretch Armstrong is."

"The person leaving the clues must know you a little, even if they're just a reader of your column, and only know you by your byline photo. Even with that it's safe to say they have a ballpark idea of how old you are. They'd know you were of a generation that would be familiar with Stretch Armstrong."

"So you're saying it's not Neil Armstrong."

Astrid smiled back at me. "No, I agree with you, I think it is Neil Armstrong. I just want you to look at the possibility as to why it could be Stretch Armstrong."

The woman could be maddening. "Okay, fine, we're in agreement that the *where* is tied in with Neil Armstrong. So, the question is, how is it tied in?"

Astrid opened her hands in a *you tell me* manner. I gritted my teeth and took a breath. "All right. I'll play the game." I looked back out at the moon that was still playing hide and seek with the clouds. "Neil Armstrong, first man on the moon."

Astrid nodded. "So, you're saying the moon was his..."

She waited for me to fill in the blank. I felt like I was on that 70s game show, Match Game. "The moon was his..." I didn't know where the hell this was going. "It was his..." Astrid tilted her head expectantly, clearly already knowing the answer but patiently waiting for me to put two and two together. "It was his destination?" She leaned in and circled her hand toward me like she was reeling in a fishing line in reverse. I kept guessing, "His goal, his end game, his stop..."

Astrid sat back. "Bingo!"

It took me a second to figure out what I'd said. "Armstrong's...stop. The moon was his stop! Like a bus stop. Where he was going."

Astrid nodded and smiled, like a teacher who's proud of their overly stupid pupil who just figured out a simple math problem. "The moon is Armstrong's stop. Now, the rest of that part of the clue. Aqua."

"Water? But there's no water on the moon."

"Who said anything about water. Does aqua only have one definition?"

"Uh, no. Let's see, aqua…the color?"

"Yea, could be the color. What color is aqua?"

"Sort of a blue-green."

"Technically it's exactly half way between blue and green on the color wheel. So, let's see where that leads us. Armstrong. Moon. Green."

I shook my head. Nothing. I glanced back out the window. The crescent was still stubbornly avoiding cloud cover. The sky was darkening and the moon was losing its orange tinge and fading toward a pale shade of… And it hit me. I looked Astrid right in the eye. "Nope. Not green. Blue. The blue moon.

Astrid nodded in approval and hit me with a Pulp Fiction quote. "Check out the big brain on Brad."

I said, looking at the note. "They specialize in *this* at the blue moon. They gotta be talking about the bar in the U District."

The Blue Moon Tavern is located right off I-5 at the 145th street exit at the west edge of the U District. It opened its doors in 1934 and has been pouring a steady stream of alcohol ever since. The Moon is by all accounts a dive bar—in the best sense—lots of wood, lots of posters and stickers of bands slapped on virtually every flat surface. And bands. Lots of bands. Music almost every night. The place boasts a colorful history, notably for being visited by counterculture heroes over the years. Legend has it that author Tom Robbins called Pablo Picasso in Italy from a pay phone but Picasso, the cheap bastard, wouldn't accept the collect call.

I thought about the wording of the clue. *They specialize in this.* What do they specialize in at the Blue Moon? For anyone who's ever been there that's pretty easy. The Blue Moon doesn't pour wussy drinks. People get drunk at the Blue Moon. I told Astrid my conclusion. She let that rattle around in her noggin for a second before giving a nod of acknowledgement. "Okay, I can buy that. So now let's see how that plays. What are synonyms for getting drunk?"

"Plowed. Tanked. Snockered. Hammered. Tipsy. Blotto."

Astrid said, "And how do any of those words play with the rest of the clue? *It will take you to the low-brow man of iron will.*"

"A plowed low-brow man of iron will. A tanked low-brow man. A snockered man. A Hammered man…"

We both looked each other and exclaimed the answer simultaneously. "The Hammered Man!"

The Hammered Man is not to be confused with the Hammering Man. The latter is a gigantic, kinetic, black metal sculpture in the silhouetted shape of a man swinging, as the name suggests, a hammer. He's 48 feet tall and weighs 13 tons. Located outside of the Seattle Art Museum, his arm slowly hammers four times a minute, 20 hours a day. The only times he doesn't pound away is from 1-5am, and appropriately enough, on Labor Day. The Hammered Man, on the other hand, is a slightly-larger-than life-sized spray-painted wooden replica of his taller namesake, but with one simple difference. Instead of raising and lowering a hammer, he raises and lowers what appears to be the shape of a beer bottle to his lips. He's set outside the Blue Moon when the weather cooperates.

Of course, the moment we both said the Hammered Man we both wondered if the Hammering Man was what we were really after. I made the first observation.

"Everyone knows about the Hammering Man; very few know about the Hammered Man."

Astrid countered just as quickly. "True, but the Hammering Man seems too obvious. And again, I can't help but think our mystery helper knows you a bit, and knows that you would be familiar with the Hammered Man."

I said, "What does that say about me?"

"It says you're more interesting than the average Joe and recognize the cooler things in life."

That's my girl.

I brought up the next issue. "If there's something waiting for us at either of these two pieces of fine art, odds are it will be at the one that's not mobile. The Hammering Man doesn't budge, while the Hammered Man is set out when it's not pouring down rain. Our helper isn't going to place whatever he's got for us right out on the sidewalk for anyone to pick up and walk away with. It will have to be hidden in some way so that a passing pedestrian doesn't do a grab and go."

Astrid thought on this for a moment. She looked out the window again. Broken clouds, but nothing dramatic. "Whatever our clue-meister has for us isn't going to be attached to the Hammered Man, or Hammering Man for that matter, it will be close by. Maybe only a few feet away, but hidden somehow. We both know where the Hammered Man is set out front of the Blue Moon, so we know where to look." She paused for a second before another thought came to her. "And another thing, the clue seems to speak to the Hammered Man. Take a look." She pushed the paper toward me. I read it again.

"It will take you to the low-brow man of iron will."

Astrid tapped a finger on the note. "Low-brow. The Hammering Man is outside of the Seattle Art Museum—highbrow. The Hammered Man is outside a dive bar. You do the math."

I held up my glass. She clinked it with hers. "Looks like you and I will be taking a trip to the moon."

By all accounts, the Blue Moon Tavern has a pretty freakin' cool sign out front. A naked woman, with arms and one bent leg strategically placed to hide any naughty bits, reclines on a neon-trimmed crescent moon. Below her, standing proudly on the sidewalk, was our friend the Hammered Man. Held upright by a couple of cinderblocks on its plywood base he was happily raising and lowering his beverage of choice. Behind him in the windows was a neon sign enlightening passers-by that Sierra Nevada beer was on tap inside at that very moment. Alongside it, another sign pitching the wares of local brewer Hales (Give 'em Hales!)

Astrid and I strolled up to the Hammered Man and tried to look around as nonchalantly as we could, which wasn't saying much. We pretty much looked like two people trying not to look like we were looking around for something. We started by checking out the Hammered Man himself but with one quick scan realized he was clean. We then turned our eyes to the façade of the bar itself. Thin bricks make up the space for the lower three feet before hitting the blue painted window sills. We poked around there for a minute. Nothing. We then moved over to the right where a two-foot wide run of standard bricks acted as a break before another window. It was here where something caught my eye. I crouched down onto my knees and peered closer at one brick in particular that seemed just ever so slightly out of whack. Upon closer inspection, I could see that it was loose, the mortar around it, missing. I glanced around to make sure I wasn't being watched and gave a whistle to Astrid who was running her hands under the window sills further down the way. She heard my signal and scampered over. I indicated toward the brick and gave it a little shake. It instantly pulled loose. I eased it out of its space, and lo and behold, behind it was something small, flat and slightly reflective. I pulled it out. It was a folded-up clear plastic sandwich bag. The ziplock kind. I held it up to Astrid and she took it from my hand. I carefully checked to see if there was anything else in the cavity behind the brick. Nothing else presented itself so I placed the brick back in its hole and practically jumped to my feet.

"What is it?" I asked.

Astrid was holding it up to the light. "Dunno." The bag had been folded over enough times so that the plastic was no longer transparent. She looked at me, expectantly. "Shall we?"

I said, "Go for it."

Astrid began unfolding the bag until the contents began to reveal themselves. When the bag was completely unfolded, she unzipped the top and reached in, pulling out a small tuft of what looked like fur. She looked a little closer at it, even smelled it, then looked to me. "What do you think?"

I took it from her and gave it a closer inspection. "Fur?"

"Looks that way."

I rubbed it between my fingers. "Almost looks and feels like that fake fur they make cheap costumes out of."

The fur was a medium brown, the sample, about the size of a fifty-cent piece. I placed it back inside the bag and tucked it inside my coat pocket.

"Who's the resident expert on all things with fur?"

Astrid nodded. "The Animal Man. What a coincidence."

The next day Astrid was on the clock so she couldn't join me but told me to let her know if I found anything. It was clear she was beginning to enjoy this mystery as much, if not more, than me.

I showed up at the Bongo Congo Kennels unannounced. I've found that showing up without warning usually yielded more promising results. Less chance for my target to take it on the heel and toe if they don't know I'm coming. But in this case, I needn't have worried; Ketchikan was more than happy to see me. He was right in the middle of feeding an excessively large snake his ration of small furry woodland creatures. He closed the lid to the large glass aquarium that acted as the snake's home.

"Hey, Fred, soup's on!" He barked at the snake.

Ketch wiped his hands on a towel and turned his attention to me. "Back again, eh? What's on your mind, Stew?"

I hated it when people called me Stew. Probably as much as Charlie Can Do hated being called Chuck. I may have to reevaluate me calling him that. I took out the baggie and handed it toward Ketchikan. "What kind of animal is this fur from?"

Ketchikan opened the bag, took one quick look and handed it back. "Two questions: Why do you want to know? And where did you get it?"

I told him that it was a clue in the story I came to see him about earlier. Then I told him about the mysterious benefactor who left it for me. He shrugged it off like that was an acceptable answer.

"The fur is from a frple. Which means it's from Ggoorrsstt."

"Ggoorrsstt? Why would someone be leaving me a lock of fur from Ggoorrsstt?"

The Animal Man grabbed his coat. "Maybe it's time we ask him."

We arrived at the city dump and headed straight to J.P.'s magic house, which was nothing more than a shack. We found his red tricycle lying on its side in the alley beside the weathered aluminum garbage can and the Dutch-door. Ketchikan didn't even bother to knock.

"J.P.'s away on business. Pretty sure he's up at the North Pole visiting Santa. He likes to do that a few months out from Christmas to see how the old guy's doing before things get really hairy for him. He likes for me to check on things for him while he's out."

We walked in and all the cluttered furnishings that I'd grown up seeing on TV were right where they always were. There was the PEEK-A-VUE on the wall: J.P.'s all-purpose monitor where he could talk with Santa or launch cartoons or commercials. To the left of the door was the black oven where Tikey Turkey slept. To the right of the door was the famous bright green I.C.U.2-TV, where J.P. would sit, spin the knobs, and see who was having a birthday, and where their presents were hidden (more likely than not, in the dryer). Across the room, watching us with those big soulful eyes was none other than Grandpa Tick Tock: The talking grandfather clock with enormous ears that make him look like a car with both front doors open.

"Hello, boys," said the clock; his voice, old and leathery. "What brings you around today?"

Ketchikan took point. "Another check on the frple, grandpa."

Grandpa Tick Tock's big eyes rolled up, down, left and right as he spoke. "He has been off his feed a bit lately. Well, good luck."

And with that the clock was silent. Ketchikan and I walked over to the door to the secret room—Ggoorrsstt's lair. Ketchikan held an arm out, blocking my path.

"Stand back. Things can get a little dicey when using the secret words."

Any kid who grew up watching J.P. Patches knew what he was talking about. More often than not, upon uttering the words, the door would fling violently open, knocking J.P. to the floor. I heeded Ketch's advice and moved back a respectable distance. Ketchikan pointed his hands at the door like he was about to cast a spell and uttered the magic words.

"Zabba-zabba-zabba-zoo, secret room, alakazoo!"

The door immediately blasted open, sending Ketchikan reeling. One of the other peculiar characteristics of opening the door is that Ggoorrsstt's unseen cousins, Patti, Maxine and

Laverne (coincidentally, the same names of the Andrew Sisters), begin chanting "Ooga-chaka, ooga-ooga-ooga-chaka", which sounds surprisingly similar to Blue Swede's 1974 hit, Hooked on a Feeling.

Seconds later Ggoorrsstt slowly dragged himself out of the secret room. Grandpa Tick-Tock was right, the frple did not look like the bright-eyed creature I'd seen on TV before. He stepped in, with his hands (paws?) on his hips, like we were infringing on his time. His body language clearly suggested serious attitude.

When Ggoorrsstt talks, it sounds something like, "Ruh-ruh-ruh-ruh", but with different pitches. When he spoke to Ketchikan it was clear he was being very direct. If a New Yorker could speak frple it would probably sound like this. Ketchikan responded and they went back and forth for a moment. Finally, Ketch turned to me. "Ggoorrsstt claims no one has come by to see him other than me and Gertrude."

I asked, "Has Gertrude come by herself?"

"Nope. I'm the only one who's come alone."

"Then how did someone get a tuft of frple fur?"

Ketchikan shrugged. "That wouldn't be that hard. Ggoorrsstt makes public appearances. He sheds."

I looked at the frple, who was still displaying physical attitude. "Does he even realize he's acting a little surly?"

Ketchikan looked the frple over. "I don't think so."

"How long has he been acting this way?"

Ketchikan rubbed his chin in thought and said, "Well, let's see, I got the first call from Gertrude about a month ago. So, it's safe to say it had to have been going on for at least a couple of weeks before then."

"So, what happened six weeks ago that could have set this off?"

We stood in silence for a moment while Ggoorrsstt wandered over to a box of frple fodder and proceeded to have a snack. I watched as he grabbed handfuls of the stuff and jammed it into his armpit and flapped his elbow against his ribs like it was a chicken wing. Evidently, that's how frples eat. I took a look at the fodder; it looked for all the world like Styrofoam packing peanuts. Then something hit me. I turned to Ketchikan.

"What was it Grandpa Tick-Tock said about Ggoorrsstt?"

Ketchikan thought for a second. "He said he thought Ggoorrsstt hadn't been feeling well."

"No, he said he's been off his feed."

116

I raced over to the box that Ggoorrsstt was eating out of and looked it over. "When was Ggoorrsstt's last delivery of frple fodder?"

Ketchikan said, "Let's see, he gets a fresh shipment every two months. Judging by what's left in that box I'd say it was right around…"

I finished his thought for him. "Six weeks ago."

I turned the box around until I found what I was looking for, the shipping label. "This shipment was from farmer Fred from Fife." I turned back to Ketchikan. "You said he gets his fodder from farmer Fred and farmer Frank from Ferndale. How does that work?"

Ketchikan said, "They alternate shipments. Fred this time, Frank the next time."

"That means farmer Frank's frple fodder will be coming in in about two weeks." I paced the room for a moment. "First, we need to determine whether farmer Fred's frple fodder is what's been causing Ggoorrsstt's change in attitude. Then we need to find out if farmer Frank's does the same thing."

Ketchikan nodded in agreement. "Do you want to wait the two weeks until the shipment comes in?"

"No. But that's all right. I hear Ferndale is beautiful this time of year."

The next day I spent the better part of the morning doing research down at the paper. Their archives are second to none. I've found things in there I couldn't even find on Google. This time around I was mining for a little frple fodder gold. On the Internet, I found a few mentions of farmers Fred and Frank and their frple fodder business, but not as much as I would have liked, so I dug into the paper's microfiche. The Analog is a new paper but worked a deal to get access to the Post Intelligencer and Times' archives. It's here that I was wading through old articles that were written long before .com ever existed. In the old days, articles and pages of newspaper were photographed and printed on tiny pieces of film which were then stored on reels. You'd then scroll through the film using a machine that simply acted as a lighting and magnifying device. The articles would be projected up onto the device screen. I found a few articles from way back when farmers Fred and Frank landed the frple fodder contracts. When Ggoorrsstt first came to Seattle to live with J.P., he was a tremendous curiosity. The Clown could have made a fortune off the frple, charging people to see him, but instead he took him in and quietly cared for him. Kind of like Willy Wonka and the Oompa

Loompas. At first J.P. was hit with a tidal wave of media requests, but he always politely declined. Over time the novelty of the frple wore off and people simply began to accept him as just another Northwest resident, albeit an unusual one.

Even though Ggoorrsstt was accepted into the community he was still undeniably exotic. And the exotic creature had exotic tastes in food. It wasn't long before J.P. realized the frple didn't eat the same things as the rest of us—Ggoorrsstt wasn't a Thai food and sushi frple—so J.P. put the job of supplying food for Ggoorrsstt out to bid. Needless to say, every food service provider in the area made a pitch. Chef Tom Douglas had his people working around the clock to come up with something to the frple's liking, but to no avail. J.P. discovered that the only thing frple's liked was frple fodder, and the only place one could get frple fodder was from Ggoorrsstt's home island of ORIK. The island isn't exactly an airline hub, so getting the fodder was insanely expensive. That's where two entrepreneurial Northwest farmers named Fred and Frank came into play.

People from throughout the region were doing their best to grow their own frple fodder, but for some reason, the local soil wasn't a good match. Time after time someone would claim to have grown the perfect fodder, only to watch as Ggoorrsstt would take one bite and spit it out.

No one has been really sure why a farmer in Fife and a farmer in Ferndale were somehow able to grow acceptable frple fodder, but theirs was the only farms that pulled off the trick. J.P. immediately bestowed upon them lifetime contracts to supply the fodder, and as a result, farmer Fred and farmer Frank's children, grandchildren and great-grandchildren will most likely be set for life.

While I was scanning through the reels of microfiche my cell phone rang. I picked it up, expecting it to be Astrid. Instead what I heard was the unmistakably high-pitched singing of "It's June in January when I'm with you." Gertrude.

I tried to play it cool, but I my heart was doing laps. It's not every day you get a call from a woman of Gertrude's caliber. Imagine a college kid getting a call from a Sports Illustrated swimsuit model. Yeah, it's something like that.

"Hello, Gertrude, what can I do for you?" I tried to play it cool.

She dove into the conversation like we were old pals. "Hi, Stewart, how are you, my dear? It's so nice to finally speak with you. I'm a huge fan. Huuuge! Love your work."

Gertrude, a fan of my work? Be still my heart. "Well thank you, Gertrude." I tried to return the old-pal vibe but I'm sure I must have sounded like a thirteen-year-old with a crush on the head cheerleader. "What can I do for you?"

"Ketchikan tells me you and he paid a visit to Ggoorrsstt and came away with some interesting thoughts on his behavior. I also understand you've been seeing similar behavior from the non-frple population."

"I have." I was so tongue-tied I didn't know what else to say. It didn't matter because she jumped right in with more.

"Well then, I have something that might be of interest to you. Who am I kidding, I know it will be of interest to you because *it is* for you."

This snapped me out of my stupor. "I'm sorry, what did you say? You have something for me?"

I could hear her rustling around on the other end of the line, like she was shuffling through papers. "I know it's around here someplace. One-moment plee-ease."

My heart almost stopped right there and then. I felt like I just heard Humphrey Bogart say *Here's looking at you, kid.* A moment later she was back on the line.

"Found it! My, my, look at this. A note. And such a lovely one."

"Wait, you have a note for me? How did you get it?"

"I found it this morning when I went out to feed my darling little pet pigs, Fred and Ethel. There it was, in all its perfect penmanship glory, addressed to you. Why something for you was left for me I have no idea, but I'm going to find out."

"Um, sure," I stammered. "Where can I pick up the note?"

"Don't be silly, Stewart, I'll bring it to you. At your paper?"

"That would be fine."

"The Analog it is. I'll see you in thirty. It's a date."

And just like that, the line was dead. I felt like I was working on a 500-piece puzzle, and right in the middle of it, someone swapped it out for a 1000-piecer.

I waited for Gertrude in the lobby, and thirty-minutes later, on the button, she came bursting in, in full-throat.

"It's June in January, when I'm with you!"

She saw me and swept across the room with a grandeur you had to witness to fully appreciate. The woman knew from making an entrance. She extended her hand, not for a shake, but more in the style of expecting me to delicately take and kiss it. I didn't. Kiss it, I mean, but boy howdy, I'd be lying if the thought didn't cross my mind for a micro-second.

There weren't many people in the lobby at that moment but the few that were there all turned to witness the glory that is Gertrude. She fills a room with her mere presence. It's virtually impossible to turn your eyes from her. They say that all the great ones have what's commonly referred to as "It", or the X-factor. You can't really describe it, but you know it when you see it. It's a charisma you're born with, that can't be learned.

For as big a personality as Gertrude is, it's a bit surprising I haven't interviewed her before. I've written about her, but never had a sit down; a blank-spot on my resume I soon expected to rectify. I wasn't sure how deeply Gertrude would weave into this story I was bird-dogging, but there was no question she was playing a role. As evidenced by the fact that she was acting as a conduit for another clue.

She took my arm and shepherded me to a pair of chairs along a side wall. With surprising strength, she inserted me into one of the chairs in a manner where it almost felt like I was doing it of my own free will. I didn't resist. She dropped into the other seat, reached across, took my chin in her hand and turned my head to face her. Anyone else does this and they get a right cross for their troubles, but Gertrude did it so matter of fact, and with such a big smile it never crossed my mind to be upset.

"So, Stewart, my dear, tell me, what are you up to? Hmm? Something juicy? Something with a big headline and legs? Ketch tells me you're working on some great mystery, and X. R. Cise says the same thing. So, tell me, tell me, tell me, what on earth could you be doing and how can it involve me?"

This was standard operating procedure for Gertrude. She craved the spotlight like a skid row wino craves a bottle of Boone's Farm Strawberry Hill. From what I understand it's been a life-long obsession for her. Born on Bainbridge Island in a devoutly theatrical family her path in life was mapped, grated, leveled and packed from an early age. Her father, an old vaudevillian who went by the stage name Iron Head Schmedlap, ran an act that featured him taking any number of shots to the kisser. As a result, before he was forty he was already getting a reputation of being, shall we say, a little off-kilter. His bit never packed them in, but it endured—it had legs. He was savvy enough to know stepping on upturned rakes or banana peels was funny a hundred years ago and will be funny a hundred years from now. He barnstormed throughout the country, latching on to traveling circuses and vaudeville troupes who needed to fill a temporary hole in their lineup. He met with Gertrude's future mom while bivouacking with a side-show in Albuquerque, New Mexico. She was a singer of a common stripe: a songbird who couldn't cut it on the big-league circuit, but good enough to pay the rent. Once the two became a couple they formed a new act, The Singing Schmedlaps. He still took the head-shots, but now to the dulcet tones of his lovely wife. It was a surprising hit and gave them a taste of what the big time could be like. They never quite crossed over to the level of Carnegie Hall but made enough headlines to give them a thirst for the A-list. The problem was, they never reached it. They were B or C-list for a cup of coffee and then, poof, the public's taste changed and they were relegated to second run shows in backwater towns. They finally read the writing on the wall and set down roots just off the coast of

Seattle. They still stayed active in the hoity-toity Bainbridge theater community but their focus was no longer on their own careers; they were bent on seeing their own progeny reach the heights that they found just out of reach.

If you look up the definition of Stage Parents in the dictionary you'll most likely see a picture of Gertrude's mom and dad. They were known far and wide as a terror to talent and casting agents. If there was a part for a girl anywhere close to Gertrude's age she had better damn well be considered for the role. She studied with every singing, acting and dancing instructor within a twenty-mile radius. And they seldom lasted. If Gertrude's parents didn't see marked improvement overnight they pulled her and enrolled her with another teacher. This would have been at least reasonably understandable except for one small problem: Gertrude had no talent. Other than an overabundance of confidence, charisma and unearthly good looks. She had her parent's ability to command an audience but not a lick of talent. She couldn't sing, couldn't dance and couldn't act her way out of wet rice-paper bag. Her parent's marginal talent gene clearly skipped a generation and they blindly refused to accept this cruel reality. Apparently so did Gertrude. There's no question she could have had a stellar career as a model, with that face and figure, but for some reason she felt that was a cop out and kept her laser-focus on competing for the stage. It wasn't until she'd aged out of the modeling game before she realized she'd missed her chance.

So now, here we were. I had a potentially blockbuster story and she was hell-bent on getting in on it as a ticket to the front page. It's not like I could deny her access; she had the next clue, so technically she was now part of the story. The question was, how much would she be involved? I asked her to see the note and with a flourish it magically appeared in her hand. I reached up to take the note and she pulled it just out of my reach. "Stewart, my boy, what's in it for me?"

Her audacity was spectacular but her question, I had to admit, was reasonable. What was in it for her? I knew damn well what she wanted, and luckily, I was in a position to grant her wish. "Your name in print, my dear Gertrude. On a front-page story. A story that will rock this town to its foundation." Her flair for the theatric was intoxicating and I found myself slipping into character. "The question, of course, is, if it's true. And the only way I'll be able to find out is if I see that note." I held my hand out.

Gertrude seemed to be weighing options in her head, still holding the note out of my reach "Hmm. Seems like I'm very important to this story. A leading role, I should say."

I stayed in character. "I should say as well. And if it comes together like I'm guessing it could, once it hits newsstands everyone will know the name of Gertrude."

Gertrude gave a musical laugh. "They already do, my dear boy, they already do. But one can't simply rest on one's laurels, now can they?"

"No, they can't."

"And so, one must constantly fan the flames of fame, as it were, wouldn't you agree?"

"I would. But without me that flame won't get fanned."

This last little rejoinder seemed to convince her and she placed the note in my hand. It was written in the same fluid cursive as the first note. I glanced at the message and back to Gertrude. "You've read it, of course?"

"Of course, but I haven't the foggiest idea as to what it could mean."

I read the note aloud. "*Take the road of Smart's counterpart to where the politically incorrect restaurant used to stand. Look below the trunk.*"

I looked back and Gertrude who was sporting a coquettish grin. She simply said, "Make sure your photographer gets my good side."

Astrid and I sat at a booth in the Northlake Tavern and pizza house, below one of the numerous David Horsey murals of people eating Northlake pizza. Dave used to be cartoonist at the PI. Swell guy; won a Pulitzer prize. The Northlake, as the name suggests, is at the very northernmost tip of Lake Union, a block off the water, between the I-5 and the Montlake bridges. When I was a kid I asked my dad, who had the best pizza in Seattle and he said the Northlake Tavern. Then when I was in high school I asked one of my teachers the same question and they gave me the same answer, so from that point on I went on the assumption that the Northlake Tavern was at the top of the pizza food-chain. To my tastes, it still is.

We were working our way through a Logger Special and chasing it with a pint of Hale's, the note sitting on the table between us. After a couple of bites, I nodded toward the note and said, "Ready for round two?"

Astrid was still jawing through a pound of cheese so she just nodded. After a swig to clear the palette she said, "You first."

I smiled at her. "I think I've got this one licked."

"Do tell."

I leaned in. "First half of the first line: *Take the road of Smart's counterpart.* The question, of course, is who or what is Smart's counterpart. To know this, we must first know who or what Smart is. Would you agree, Dr. Watson?"

"Indeed, I would, Mr. Holmes."

"So," I said, "I feel it is safe to say that Smart is a who, not a what."

"Based on what?"

"Gut feeling."

"I can go with that."

"I'm glad you approve. So, who do we know named Smart? The two that jump to mind: the actress Jean Smart, and, of course, Maxwell Smart, Agent 86. Who do you think is more logical?"

Astrid thought for a second and said, "Maxwell Smart is more fun, but Jean Smart makes more sense."

"Pray tell, why?"

"She's local. Went to the UW, began her career doing regional theater around here before hitting it big on Designing Women."

"I completely agree with you. Jean Smart is the logical choice. But it's the wrong one."

"And you feel this because..."

"Because it's the logical choice. Our clue-meister is a sharp guy, or gal, and, I'm guessing, is having fun putting this game together. Jean Smart, because she's got local roots, is the fastball. Maxwell Smart is the curveball."

"So why do you think Max is the clue?"

I took a sip of the Hale's. "Let's first start with Jean and how she would relate to the rest of that sentence. We're looking for Smart's counterpart. Who would you consider Jean Smart's counterpart?"

"It would have to be one of the other actresses on Designing Women," said Astrid. "Julia Sugarbaker, played by Dixie Carter, Suzanne Sugarbaker, played by Delta Burke, or Mary Jo Shively, played by Annie Potts."

"How the hell do you know that?"

"Designing Women, Murphy Brown, back to back. That was my must-see-TV at that time."

"Okay, fine. My next question is, are there any local roads with those names?"

"Prominent ones? I would say no."

"As would I. So, then we move to Maxwell Smart, secret agent extraordinaire, who worked for CONTROL, a secret U.S. government counter-intelligence agency constantly doing battle with KAOS, the international organization of evil."

"I can guess what your must-see-TV was back in the late 60s. Keep going."

"You're a *smart* girl—heh, heh—I think you can put it together."

"Sorry, wasn't as big a fan as you. Connect the dots for me."

"Fine. Maxwell Smart was agent 86. His partner, played by Barbara Feldon, was…wait for it…99." I sat back and threw my hands out, sort of like, Ta-da!

Astrid smiled. "99. Aurora Avenue." She held up her beer, I tapped it with mine. "Well done."

I was on a roll so I kept going. "Second half of the first line: *To where the politically incorrect restaurant used to stand*. There have been a lot of restaurants on Aurora over the years but I can only think of two that could come even close to being considered politically incorrect."

"And those would be…"

"Let's start south and make our way north. The first would be right around the north end of Green Lake. It was tough to miss; two big old teepees, side by side."

"Sure. The Twin Teepees. They had good Eggs Benny."

"Good call. Yes, they did. The place was razed back in 2000. Had been around for over 60 years. Harland Sanders, the Kentucky Fried Chicken founder, worked there."

"He did not."

"He did so. Or so the story goes. In fact, the story also goes that he perfected his fried chicken recipe in the Twin Teepees kitchens, but nobody can prove it. But I digress. I wouldn't exactly call the Twin Teepees politically incorrect, even by Seattle's liberal standards."

"So, what's the other restaurant that might fit the bill?"

"It's a beauty. Head north a couple of minutes and there used to stand a chain restaurant called Sambos."

"Oh my God, that's right! I forgot about Sambos."

"Sambo: as in, racist slur. Sambo: as in, the book *The Story of Little Black Sambo*, the dark-skinned South Indian boy. I did a little reading. This is awesomely ridiculous. The restaurant chain name was derived from the two owner's names: Sam—for Sam Battistone Sr. and Bo for Newell Bohnett. But they totally played up the Little Black Sambo connection. There were paintings of the character all over the restaurant. The restaurant's original mascot was even a dark-skinned South Indian Boy."

"I don't see that flying today."

"Ah, no. There were 1,117 Sambos restaurants across the country. They were huge!"

"And now they're all gone."

"Not quite. There's still one left, the original, down in Santa Barbara, California."

"Weird."

"No kidding. So, there you have it, Sambos, the politically incorrect restaurant on 99." I did the Ta-da thing again with my hands.

"So, what's the last part about? *Look under the trunk?*"

"That I'm not so sure about yet. I don't know if there's a tree there now or what. Let us repair to 99 for a look-see, shall we?"

"We shall."

While standing at the corner of N 88th and Aurora we knew exactly what the last part of the clue meant. The old Sambos structure still stands but is now the home of Aurora Rents. The building just to the north, which is now also part of Aurora Rents, used to be a flower shop. What made the flower shop such a recognizable Seattle fixture over the years, wasn't the shop itself, but the object sitting in front, on two steel posts, about fifteen feet off the ground: an elephant.

There are two iconic elephants in Seattle: The neon Pink Elephant sign for the Elephant Car Wash, downtown, and the gray elephant statue above the old Aurora Flower shop. The latter has a more interesting history.

The life-sized pachyderm was first created by mosaic craftsman John Giovanni Braida to plug his tile business in Fremont. He had his staff work on it for the better part of ten years to keep his employees busy during the Great Depression. Braida wanted the elephant to look as grand as possible, and took his inspiration from the elephants of India. He even had his people put a howdah—a decorative carriage—on the elephant's back.

The elephant was made of concrete spread over chicken wire, stretched over a frame. The elephant

137

was completed in the mid-30s and kept watch over Braida's business until 1946, when the elephant was sold to the owner of the Aurora Flower shop for the princely sum of $500. Fast forward 60-some years and the poor elephant was, quite literally, on his last legs. Pigeons had taken up home inside his belly and he was in severe disrepair. It was time to fix him up or tear him down. Luckily the decision was made by the Aurora Rents owner to refurbish the icon, and thousands of dollars later, the elephant had a complete facelift.

If I haven't mentioned it yet, elephants have trunks. Clue solved.

Astrid and I paced around the base of the columns holding up the elephant, searching for something that looked out of place. We found it under a good-sized rock resting beside the telephone pole that stood between the elephant and the street. The problem was, we didn't know what we'd just found.

Under the rock, and partially buried was a plastic bag. There was something inside that appeared at first glance like the corpse of some dead animal, but upon closer inspection was a toy stuffed animal, the kind kids play with, like a Teddy Bear, except this one wasn't a bear. I took it out of the bag and turned it around and around in my hands, looking it over. Definitely not a bear. I held it up to Astrid. "What do you think of this?"

She took it from my hands and did the same rotating around thing to look at it from all angles. "It's a bat."

"What kind of kid wants to snuggle up with a bat?"

"Beats me. And why is there a bell around its neck?"

I smiled. "Finally, a clue that doesn't take forever to figure out. A bat. A bell. What do bells do?"

"Ring?"

"Sorry, what sound do bells make?"

"Ding?"

"And we put it together…"

"Ding. Bat" Her eyes lit up. "Dingbat! Dingbatman!"

I touched my index finger to my nose. "On the nosey! Our clue-meister wants us to find Dingbatman."

Astrid said, "Well, he always has always been an arch nemesis of Boris S. Wort and Zenobia (gasp). He's foiled their nefarious plots on more than one occasion."

We both stopped and thought for a moment. We looked at each other with the same lost expression. I chimed in first with the question that was clearly pestering both of us. "So how exactly do we find Dingbatman?"

"Google search?"

"You think he has a website?"

"I dunno. Maybe. Stranger things have happened."

We both whipped out our phones simultaneously and began tapping away. Almost at the same time, we called out, "Found it!"

Astrid squinted at her screen. "At least I think this is it." She started reading the webpage. "Dingbatman. Local hero to the oppressed. Vanquisher of evil. Available for parties. Reasonable rates."

I looked at the same website on my own phone. "The guy couldn't get his site done professionally? There must be a dozen spelling errors on his home page. Good grief."

"Well, he is a dingbat."

"Good point. Do you see a phone number?"

Astrid scrolled through the site. "No phone number, just a contact form."

"I hate contact forms."

"Me too. But no worries, I think I might know someone who can help us out." I cleared my phone, punched in a phone number, and put it on speaker. Within seconds both Astrid and I heard the unmistakable sound of...

"One-moment plee-ease!"

Astrid looked up at me in surprise. I held my hand up in a *I got this* gesture, and spoke into the phone. "Gertrude. Stewart Street here."

My phone nearly jumped out of my hand with Gertrude's reply. The woman could project. "Stewart, darling, how are you?"

"I'm well, Gertrude. New information on the story I was telling you about," I knew just how to hook her, "requiring more help from you."

You could hear Gertrude's voice puff up with pride. "Well, I'm certainly becoming important to your story, aren't I? Becoming leading lady status, wouldn't you say?"

"Could be, Gertrude. Look, I'm trying to track down Dingbatman, but I can't find a phone number. You have any idea how to reach him?"

"Do I? Well of course! Dingy and I go way back. We used to be a thing, don't you know. Moonlit dinners at the Needle, Sunday picnics at the Locks. Goodness, how that man could sweep a woman off her feet."

"But I thought you and J.P…"

"Came later. Dingy and I lit the torch when I was still just an ingénue. He came to see me when I was still just a chorus girl at a Bainbridge Island production of West Side Story. Want to hear me trill my Rs?"

"Another time, maybe."

"Dingy was there for every performance. Six nights straight." I could hear a wistfulness in Gertrude's voice, harkening back to her not-quite-glory days. "A bouquet of white roses in my dressing room after every show." She let out a deep sigh. "What a man."

"Uh, Gertrude. Dingbatman's phone number?"

She snapped out of her revelry. "I can't give out his direct number but I'd be happy to connect you. One-moment plee-ease."

I had to admit, it was kind of cool being connected using an old-school operator. A few clicks later and I was listening to the winged warrior himself. "Dingbat man, here. Friend of the friendless, defender of the defenseless, ally of the working man and bushwhacker of baddies. What can I do for you?"

That high, sing-songy, almost cartoonish voice I'd heard numerous times on TV belted out of the phone's tiny speaker. Even after so many years as a columnist I still got star-struck on occasion.

"Uh, hello, Dingbatman, my name is Stewart Street and I need your help." I gave him a reader's digest version of what was going on and about the bat stuffy. He took it all in without interruption until I was finished.

"Funny you should be calling me. I think I have something for you."

Astrid and I locked eyed. I asked, "What do you have?"

"Tell you what, Street. Meet me at the top of the Space Needle, observation deck, 5pm sharp. I'll tell you then."

142

And the line went dead.

The Space Needle observation deck is the place that everyone not from Seattle goes when they visit Seattle. Locals make the trip, pretty much only when they're showing off the sights to visiting friends and relatives.

The Space Needle is the world's biggest tripod. Six hundred and five feet straight up, with a flying saucer perched on top. It's one of the few buildings on the planet that is intrinsically linked to its home city. Honestly, how many can you think of? The Eifel Tower, the Empire State Building, the Leaning Tower. It's a short list.

Two countries outside the United States actually had a significant influence on the creation of the Space Needle: Russia and Germany. In 1957, the Soviets shocked the world by launching the world's first satellite, *Sputnik*. The space race was on! And courtesy of that race, Seattle's upcoming world's fair suddenly had a theme: Space. Consider that influence number one. Influence number two came a couple of years later when the chairman of the Washington State World's Fair Commission, while traveling abroad, was having dinner with his wife in a restaurant that was perched atop a television transmission tower in Stuttgart, Germany. He sketched out his own version of a space age looking tower on a place mat and mailed it back home. Before long the wheels of invention were turning, and just like that, Seattle had a symbol for its upcoming 1962 World's Fair. But there was just one, tiny little question they still hadn't considered: Could it be built?

In the fall of 1960, with less than 18 months before the fair, there was no definitive building site for the Needle, no final design, and no bank loan guarantee. No problem! A piece of land was eventually secured on the fairground site that would have been barely big enough to hold a baseball diamond (only 120' x 120') and bought for seventy-five thousand dollars. The local banks, which had been balking at loaning the money necessary to build the Needle, eventually coughed up the 4.5 million needed to build it. To put things in perspective, Safeco Field, the baseball stadium that the Seattle Mariners call home was built in 1999 at the slightly higher price of four *hundred* million dollars. There are homes on the outskirts of Medina that would go for 4.5 mill.

The Needle touts a 540-degree view. How? Stand in the gift shop and look up. Glass ceiling. There's your other 180 degrees. Marketing, baby.

While you're standing at the base of the Space Needle, craning your neck like the countless tourists and Seattleites before you, one thought invariably runs through your head: What if it tips over? As they like to say in that little town over on the east coast…*Fuhgedaboudit*. Four hundred and sixty-seven truckloads of concrete (5,600 tons) in the foundation have ensured that the Space Needle's center of gravity is right about level with your head. It's been designed to withstand winds of up to two hundred miles an hour and an earthquake would have to rank somewhere along the lines of, oh, say, massive and catastrophic to even put a hitch in the Needle's giddyap.

Once you climb on board the elevator and take a ride on up to the business end of the Needle you've got a couple of options. Let me skip past the restaurant level for a moment to touch briefly on the observation deck. A finer view of Seattle and the surrounding area you simply will not find. If it's a clear day *(Ha, ha, ha)* you will be able to see hundreds of miles in every direction. Interestingly enough, while in the design phase the guys drawing up the Needle's dimensions took a helicopter ride above the spot where the Space Needle was going to be built and discovered there was no reason to build it higher than six-hundred feet. The view wasn't any better at eight or nine-hundred feet, and at six-hundred feet you were still low enough to see everything close at hand.

Now, back downstairs for a bite at arguably the most unique eating experience you'll hope to have: The Sky City restaurant. What makes Sky City a cut above any other restaurants with a view is that this view changes while you eat: The restaurant rotates 360-degrees every hour, powered by a 1.5 horsepower electric motor. Of course, back in 1962 when the restaurant first opened for business the whole rotating restaurant thing caused a few unforeseen problems. Like patrons getting up from their table to go to the restroom only to come back and not be able to find their table. Same thing happened to the wait staff. They'd take an order and by the time they picked up the food their table had rotated to another part of the restaurant. How'd they fix the problem? Take a stroll around the restaurant, you'll notice that it's divided up into four sections, each subtly color-coded.

Over the years, the Space Needle has played host to more celebrities, royalty, and bigwigs than you can shake a stick at. Let's just say, if the Space Needle was cool enough for Elvis to want to make a movie here *(It Happened at the World's Fair)* then it was obviously cool enough for the likes of presidents and assorted captains of industry. In fact, legend has it that way back when, a young boy of fourteen, as a reward from his pastor for memorizing and reciting the Sermon on the Mount, won a trip to the Space Needle restaurant. No doubt the experience helped bolster the boy's confidence, leading him on the path that eventually took him to co-founding a little local company called Microsoft and made him the richest person on planet Earth. Hey, if a simple trip to the Space Needle can do that for a guy like Bill Gates, imagine what it can do for you.

But today I wasn't here to gnosh. I had a date with Dingbatman.

I strolled out onto the observation deck and was immediately hit with reason number 1,328 as to why I do so love it here. As they say on the Space Needle website, at 520 feet, nothing blocks you from a 360-degree panorama of the Emerald City. The autumn sun was glinting off a thousand skyscraper windows while a few random clouds hung quietly overhead. The Cascade mountains to the east, and Olympics, across the sound to the west, stood sentry, the top most reaches of their peaks perpetually white with snow, like some titan baker had gotten busy with a bag of flour and sifter.

The observation deck is completely caged in. I guess they think a manic depressive taking a header off the deck might be bad for business. There weren't many visitors at the moment. Drop by in the summer, however, and it's a whole different ball game. Tourist central. As I slowly worked my way around the circumference I could hear some construction work up around the bend. Didn't sound like anything heavy duty. As I came around I could hear the contented whistling of the worker before I saw him. And before I saw him I saw something

149

else that tipped me off: A hole. Big and black, a good two feet across, with the top half of a ladder sticking up out of it, right in the middle of the walk way. And there, working on the wire fencing was Leroy Frump.

I gave him a holler and wave. He turned, saw me and his face lit up with that goofus smile. "Hey there, mithter Street! What brings you up here?"

"Enjoying the sights, Leroy. How about yourself? A little repair work, I see."

Leroy looked his handiwork over, hands on hips, looking for all the world like an even dumber version of Forrest Gump. "Uh, yep." He broke away from his quick inspection and turned back to me, eyes wide. "Have you had any more luck with your big story, mithter Street? Huh, have you? Like I said, I'm here to help, any way I can. Yeth thir ree bob."

That sound you hear is the single digit IQ rattling around inside Leroy's head.

"I'm okay, Leroy. In fact, I'm here to meet with someone who thinks they might have a clue for me."

Leroy clapped his hands to his mouth before leaning in, conspiratorially. "Who is it?"

I leaned back in. Why not give him the full cloak and dagger treatment? I whispered, "Dingbatman."

Leroy's eyes nearly popped from his skull. He slapped a meaty hand to his thigh and gave out a whoop before catching himself and covered his mouth again. "Dingbatman? For real? Wow!" He looked around, like he was making sure nobody was watching and whispered, "Can I meet him?"

I smiled good-naturedly and placed a paternal hand on his shoulder. "Absolutely." I looked around. "If he shows up, I mean."

At that moment, a voice, part fingernails on chalkboard, part high-pitched annoying sing-song, sounded behind me, and over my head. "I always show up!"

I turned to look, and there was Dingbatman, in all his glory, standing on the Space Needle roof, looking down on us through the chicken-wire.

Dingbat man isn't the most intimidating super hero. In fact, if you forgot the fact that he'd foiled numerous plots by Boris and Zenobia (gasp), he'd be hard to take seriously. I mean, just look at him. How he manages to fly with those cardboard wings is nothing short of a minor miracle. Boeing must be involved somehow. They look like they were made by a palsied five-year-old with dull scissors and masking tape. His helmet, equally cardboard, spray painted yellow, with a long, pointed beak, and dark, round sunglasses perched on the bridge—well, let's just say the look doesn't exactly instill confidence. And the kicker, of course, are the knee-length, red and white polka-dot boxers that he wears *over* his gray sweats. It's a look all right.

To my right, Leroy stared, slack-jawed and starstruck. I stared and waited for Dingbatman to get on with it. He continued to hold his pose, possibly for the tourist couple who rounded the corner, camera at the ready. They snapped off a few photos and pointed like people who have never seen a cardboard-festooned super hero standing on the roof of a fifty-story tourist attraction. Eventually Dingbatman broke his pose and cut to the chase. "I have something for you."

"So you say. What is it?"

Dingbat man kneeled down and passed a small card through a break in the chicken-wire. "A note."

I jumped up to grab the paper. Instantly, Leroy was hovering over my shoulder trying to get a peak. "Whathit say?"

I flicked him a glance of annoyance—not that he would pick up on the social cue—and turned my eyes to the note. Again, the handwriting was flawless. *"Look for the Cuban heel and vaquero chapeau where Premium Tex used to earn his dough."*

Leroy bobbed up and down on his toes, hardly containing his excitement. "Whathit mean, mithter Street? Huh?"

I slipped the note inside my pocket and shook my head. "No idea, Leroy. At least for now." I turned my attention to the super hero perched above me. "Dingbatman, who gave you this note and how did you know it was for me?"

"I found it at my aerie."

"Seriously? You live in an aerie?"

He gave a nonplussed shrug, "My apartment. Whatever. It was slipped under the door. On the envelope it came in was written, *Give to Stewart Street.* So here I am, giving it to you."

"I don't get it. Somebody keeps slipping me clues, but they always provide them to me through a third party. Weird." I thought for a moment. Why Dingbatman? If the clue-meister wants me to figure this thing out by leaving a trail of bread crumbs, why get these other people involved? And then it hit me. I said aloud, "Deep Throat."

Both Leroy and Dingbat man spoke in unison. "Excuse me?"

I looked at Leroy and then to Dingbatman. "Like in the Watergate investigation. The Washington Post reporters, Bob Woodward and Carl Bernstein, got help from a secret source who wanted to remain anonymous."

"How mythteriouth!" lisped an ecstatic Leroy.

Dingbatman said, "We good here? If there's nothing else, I must be off to make the streets of Seattle safe from ne'er to wells, riffraff, and scoundrels."

My mind was racing. I mumbled in his general direction, "Yea, yea, you do that," before pacing in a small circle.

"Wow! Dingbatman, right here in front of us! Can you believe that mithter Street?" said Leroy.

I snapped back to the now. "What? Oh yea, Dingbatman, very impressive, very cool. Look, I gotta go, Leroy. Good to see you again." And I started hoofing it for the elevator back down.

Leroy, still smiling like a kid who'd just won a year's supply of Fruit Loops, called after me. "Good luck, mithter Street! Call me anytime you need me!"

I needed to regroup and map out my next steps, so I defaulted to my tried and true method of centering myself—I called Astrid and searched out an appropriate watering hole.

We agreed to meet at yet another of our faves, the George and Dragon in Fremont. Picking a favorite drinkery in Fremont is akin to choosing a favorite flavor of ice cream; you really can't go wrong, no matter what you choose. The Red Door, the Backdoor, the Lamplighter, the High Dive. You could hit a bar a night and not run out for a month.

It was a busy night in Fremont and parking spots came dearly, as usual. I wasn't worried about having to hoof it a few blocks so when I found a vacant space near the Rocket, I snapped it up.

The Rocket is a gloriously phallic, and appropriately unique landmark relic of the 1950s cold war, bolted to a quaint little shop at the corner of Evanston and 36th. Fifty-three feet of commie retribution. It never saw active duty and received a second lease on life decorating the outside of AJ's war surplus store in Belltown. When the store went belly up in the early 90s the good folks of the Fremont Business Association stepped in and saved the rocket. By 1994 it had its new home in the Center of the Universe. The rocket fuselage is slate gray and adorned with stylish fins, giving it a more Buck Rogers vibe than it ever had in its military career. It even bears the Fremont crest and motto, "De Libertas Quirkas", which means Freedom to be Peculiar. Apropos of this neck of the woods.

The rocket is quite a sight. Except right then and there, it wasn't, and hadn't been for quite a while. The entire structure was draped in some billowy fabric that was softly flapping in the breeze. For months, some sort of construction or maintenance had been underway. A couple of men were on a scissor-lift under the base, half their bodies obscured by the fuselage. Another man was on the attached building roof, tinkering with the rocket through an opening in the silky draping. I crossed the street to make inquiries.

A short whistle caught the attention of one of the guys on the scissor-lift. He leaned down, wrench in hand to get a better look at me. I nodded at the rocket and said, "What's up?"

The dude was sort of a sketchy looking character in greasy cotton overalls. He squinted down at me and gave a shrug. "Annual maintenance and refurbishing, man. Gotta make sure she don't snap her mountings and fall on some poor schmuck."

I said, "Seems like it's been going on forever. How hard is it to tighten a few bolts and polish up this old wreck?"

The guy smiled and said, "You'd be surprised."

I pointed up at the billowy stuff. "What's with the cloaking device?"

The sketchy guy grabbed a handful of the stuff and looked up at the rocket. "Sandblasting. New paint job. Don't want to be painting civilians and passing cars."

I nodded my approval, told them to keep up the good work and turned north for my evening's destination.

The George and Dragon, or the G&D, as it is affectionately called, is a very UK pub. It's not a place you order a white wine. Frankly, I don't even know if they serve wine; I'm too chicken to ask. The G&D serves pints of beer in which you can stand a fork. You come here to watch footy (soccer), eat chips (french fries), flirt with birds (girls) and hang with blokes (guys). On this occasion, Shepherd's pie and Kronenberg 1664 lager were the order of the day for the Street table. On the telly, Chelsea and West Ham United were engaged in a nil-nil barnburner.

Astrid popped in at mid-pint and I flagged down the barkeep. Seconds later a Guinness materialized at our table. Astrid asked, "What did you learn?"

"I learned that Leroy Frump is the most employed man in Seattle."

"You ran into Leroy at the Space Needle?"

"Repairing the wire fencing around the observation deck. You should have seen him when Dingbatman arrived. It was like a kid in a candy store."

Astrid smile. She always had a soft spot for Leroy. "That's sweet. So, what did Dingbatman have for you?"

I placed the card on the sticky table between us and read the clue. "Look for the Cuban heel and vaquero chapeau where Premium Tex used to earn his dough."

Astrid made a cute face. "How poetic. Any idea?"

"Not yet. You?"

She looked it over, bit her lip, looked up at the rafters and said, "Got it."

"Really? That was fast. What does it mean?"

"I have no idea. Okay, I do have an idea. My idea is to Google it."

I smiled and took a hit off my lager. "Cheater. But my kind of cheater. Let's look."

We both whipped out our phones and started punching madly. I said, "I'll look up Cuban heel, you look up vaquero chapeau."

Astrid stopped mid-punch. "Oh, hell, what am I doing, I know what a Cuban heel is."

"Pray tell."

"It's a style of heel on boots. Mostly cowboy boots."

158

I set my phone down and chuckled. "I don't know what a vaquero is, but I'm at least sharp enough to know what a chapeau is."

"Hat."

"Yep. And I'll bet you ten of my French fries…"

"Chips, in here."

"Whatever. I'll bet you a vaquero is a cowboy."

A few quick keystrokes and Astrid held her phone out toward me. I read the words on the screen. "In Spanish-speaking parts of the U.S., a vaquero is a cowboy."

We both almost simultaneously blurted out, "Hat and Boots."

I slouched back on my bench. "Damn. That was easy. I think our clue-meister must be getting lazy."

"Either that or he is getting impatient and wants you to get to the bottom of this fast. I'm sensing a little urgency."

I looked at the clue again. "So, who's Premium Tex?"

Astrid got busy on her phone again. Within seconds she was nodding. "Got it. The Hat and Boots is a famous landmark south of Seattle, originally part of a cowboy-themed gas station built in 1954 named "Premium Tex." So there you go."

I took that in and deliberated over several fingerfuls of fries, I mean chips, and a few swigs of the 1664. "Okay, so we know where our next clue is. We still have to pay a visit to farmers Fred and Frank in Fife and Ferndale."

"Correction. *You* still have to visit them. I don't have the luxury of vanishing from my desk for days on end, like some columnists I know."

She was right. I'd hardly darkened the door of the Analog in days. Technically I'm supposed to bang out three columns a week, but I'd put in a request with my editor to take some time off when I started sniffing this story out. I figured I had another day or two before I needed to get back to the salt mine.

"I've got an idea," I said. "How about we divide and conquer? I'll zip up to farmer Frank's in Ferndale while you check out the Hat and Boots."

Astrid thought on that for a moment. "Okay, that makes sense. When are you going to head north?"

"First thing tomorrow."

"Then I'll hit the Hat and Boots tomorrow after work."

I hoisted my pint and waited for Astrid to respond in kind. "We're getting closer. I can feel it. Cheers."

The moment we clinked glasses Chelsea slipped one past the West Ham keeper in the 86th minute and the place erupted in equal parts elation and dismay.

Ferndale, Washington is about a two-hour straight shot up I-5, six miles north of Bellingham, nestled near the shores of the Nooksack River. Officially incorporated in 1907, Ferndale originally bore the name of Jam, Washington, apparently due to its proximity to a logjam on the river. Eventually, the city was renamed Ferndale by the town school teacher who apparently had a thing for ferns.

Ferndale is famous for approximately two things. It's the stomping grounds of former UW Husky and Tennessee Titans quarterback Jake Locker, and you can find homes for under $250,000. That's really about it.

One thing Ferndale does have, though, are farms. Lots of farms. And I was pulling into one of those farms at that very moment.

Like everything else I'd come across in Ferndale, farmer Frank's spread was classic rural America. A short dirt road broke away from the paved route I'd been cruising on since exiting I-5 and led me to the farm. The first thing to greet me was Frank's living quarters, a long, low rambler with beige vinyl siding, which was all the rage in the 80s. A sensible sedan that once may have been dark blue, pre-oxidation, sat outside in the cluttered carport. An overweight chocolate lab lay out front

161

and was clearly not interested in giving me the time of day. I suspect nothing short of a porterhouse would rouse the mutt from his spot.

I drove past the requisite rusted, broken-down tractor to the barn which wallowed a good fifty yards beyond. It was a hulking beast of a building, all bright red with white trim like it had just received a good coat of Sherwin-Williams before winter hit. I pulled up outside the open barn doors and climbed out. I hadn't made it three steps before farmer Frank walked out to greet me. Attention all casting agents: If you're looking for a farmer that looks like a farmer then look no further than farmer Frank. He was easily into his 80s, bent, but ambling along at a pace that showed this was a man in no hurry for anything. He was wiping his hands on his brown canvas bib overalls before reaching up to tip his tattered baseball cap back a smidge to get a better view of his unexpected guest. A Mariners cap, natch. Judging by the yellow trident logo over blue, a late 70's purchase.

He looked me over, and apparently not seeing anything to warrant a red flag, offered me a shake, which I took. "Kin I help ya?" His voice a friendly tenor.

"I sure hope so," I said. I told him I was a writer working on a story for the Analog, which earned me a nod of approval. Clearly, he was still of the generation that held some esteem for the written word and most likely started his day with a cup of coffee and a leisurely read of the daily paper. He asked what the story was about. I told him I couldn't go into details, but suffice it to say frple fodder played a role. This didn't seem to faze him much. He just gave another silent nod, waiting for me to go on. I told him I was doing research on the fodder and was hoping he might be able to give me a quick 101 on the subject.

He smiled and shook his head. "Can't imagine why anyone would care about that, but what do I know? Sure, c'mon 'round back and I'll show you what I've got."

We walked around back of the barn and headed out to the back forty. It was a pretty huge piece of farmland. I didn't see a fence but I could get a sense of where the property changed hands based on where his crops ended. It was clear that he grew a variety of different crops; the texture and color changed every couple of hundred yards. A dirt road bisected the farm into two halves with the right side dedicated to rows of I have no idea. It was clearly out of season and had been plowed under. At the time, it looked like a field of neatly aligned rows of dirt. The left side was another matter. Farmer Frank clearly didn't make all his money raising frple fodder, but was obviously a major player in the pumpkin business. And what pumpkins! As we walked among them I was struck by their size and sheer numbers. Thousands upon thousands of them, and they all seemed to be twice the size of any pumpkins I'd ever seen. They were huge! And still a lot of them. Didn't seem like he'd harvested the majority yet. Farmer Frank didn't seem to notice my gawking at his pumpkins and quietly led me through them to where the frple fodder grew. There was a clear demarcation between the pumpkins and the fodder. Pumpkins, orange; the frple fodder, a dark gray, almost black.

As we walked among the pumpkins I finally had to comment. "Excuse me, Famer Frank, but is it my imagination or are these pumpkins larger than normal?"

Farmer Frank glanced around at the orange monstrosities and gave a smile and a nod. "Ayup."
And that was the extent of his answer.

Before I could pester him some more we crossed the line to the fodder field and he stopped. Farmer Frank plunged his big hands into his overall pockets and did a slow turn "So this here would be the frple fodder. Not much ta look at."

He was right on that account. Rows and rows of dark leafy vegetation. From where I was standing it looked like the fodder grew much like carrots. I could see tufts of dark, spindly stocks popping up every foot or two. Farmer Frank reached down and grabbed one and wrestled it out of the ground. They were indeed very much like carrots, but instead of a cluster of orange finger-shaped veggies, the fodder was white and looked for all the world like Styrofoam packing peanuts. And it was a hefty amount dangling from the stocks, more than I would have guessed. Farmer Frank held it up for me to see and shook off the soil. I reached over and touched it. It even felt like packing peanuts. Farmer Frank looked it over and then turned his rheumy eyes on me. "That would be it, in all its glory. Ain't much to look at, but she pays the bills."

I snapped off a couple of the fodder and took a sniff. Nothing. No scent at all, from what I could tell. Farmer Frank got a chuckle out of that. "Odd, right? No smell. Take a taste."

He saw my eyebrows go up with a bit of trepidation and smiled back at me. "No, really, give it a try." He snapped one off, wiped it on a marginally clean spot on his overalls and handed it over. I took it gingerly and gave it another sniff. Farmer Frank gave another chortle. "Don't worry, they don't taste bad. Fact of the matter, they don't taste like nothin', really."

I placed it on the tip of my tongue. Nothing. I took a little nibble. Still nothing. I popped the fodder in my mouth and started chewing. The texture, true to form, felt pretty much just like I would imagine Styrofoam packing peanuts would feel like. And farmer Frank was right, they didn't taste like anything. Bland as can be. I spit out the

165

fodder and looked up at farmer Frank. "And yet frples think this is the best thing in the world."

"The only thing they'll eat."

"And you and farmer Fred in Fife are the only ones who grow it."

"Ayup."

"Lucky you."

"Ayup."

"Wouldn't this be considered a monopoly?"

Farmer Frank stuck his thumbs in his bib overalls and splayed his fingers out like he was some sort of big wheeler-dealer. "Technically, a monopoly would be if only one of us was selling. Ain't no laws against duopolies."

He had a point.

I looked over his fields. "When's the season?"

Farmer Frank smiled even bigger. "There ain't no season with frple fodder. Grows year 'round. And don't seem to be affected by heat nor cold. Sturdy little suckers."

I said, "You're getting ready to deliver another batch to the Clown in a couple of weeks, correct?"

"Ayep. It's my turn. Farmer Fred had the last run."

I looked at the frple fodder and said, "Have you harvested the frple you're going to send? I guess what I'm trying to ask is, how fresh is the fodder?"

Farmer Frank said, "Both Fred and I know that the frple only eats fresh fodder, so we don't cut it until a day or two before we ship it. Don't get much fresher'n that."

I looked at the fodder in his hand again. "That's a pretty hefty amount from one plant. Are they all normally this big?"

Farmer Frank looked out over his crop and I could see him rolling his tongue around in his cheek. "Funny you should mention that. Biggest crop I ever had." He held up the cluster of fodder and gave it a shake. "Each of these are probably twice the size they normally grow. Not that I'm complainin' or nuthin'."

I looked up and down the rows of frple fodder and then turned my eyes to the gigantic pumpkins. "What about your pumpkins? Have they always been this big?"

Farmer Frank shook his head. "Nope. Biggest punkins I ever grew either."

I said, "Any idea why?"

"Oh sure, gotta be the new fertilizer I been usin'."

"New fertilizer?"

"Ayep. Been usin' the same stuff for as long as I can remember and never had any complaints. Then along comes this feller a few months back and he's tellin' me he's got somethin' that'll grow my crop twice normal size. Well, I gotta tell ya, I figured him for a snake oil salesman, all talk, no sand. But he made quite a case and even left some with me for a trial run, and danged if it didn't do exactly like he said. I could hardly believe my eyes. When he came back a couple of months later I bought the whole kit 'n caboodle and ever since my frple fodder and punkins been growin' like gangbusters. My client's been thrilled."

"Who was this salesman? What was the name of his company?"

The old man doffed his cap and scratched his head. "I can't recall the feller's name, nor the company. Don't quite remember stuff as I used to. I 'spect it'll come to me eventually."

I could see this well was just about dry so I thanked farmer Frank for his time, handed him my business card and told him to give me a call if he remembered the name of the fertilizer company. We slowly ambled back toward the barn.

Just as I was getting into my car the old man shouted one last thing my way. "You gonna visit farmer Fred down in Fife as well?"

I said I would and the old man said, "Maybe he'll remember the fertilizer feller's name. He uses him too."

He gave me a wave and I pulled back out onto the main drag. The fat lab hadn't budged.

While I was in the car I gave Astrid a call. She said she'd been down at the Hat and Boots and had indeed found another clue. I asked what it was. She said, "It was, again, a meticulously handwritten note. It reads, *If at first you don't succeed in figuring out this clue, try, try, try a triangle*."

A short clue. Not a whole lot to go on, and I told her as much. I then told her what I'd learned from farmer Frank and said I was heading south and would be back home around dinner time. "Want to meet me at Jules Mae's for a bite and clue-cracking?"

"No Canlis?"

"Can't afford it."

"Jules then, huh? Going seriously old school on me."

She wasn't kidding. It doesn't get any older school than Jules Mae's. In fact, some people say it's the oldest bar in Seattle. Some say that's a bunch of crap. Astrid said she's meet me there after she was off the clock. If I was on my second round by then, so be it.

"Just don't tip too many that you can't think straight," she said, "I want to put this clue to bed before *I* go to bed. See ya 'round, Street."

I merged into traffic and settled in for the long haul south.

Jules Mae's is an interesting place with an interesting back story. It's an old-timey bar of the first order. Signs prominently boast "Since 1888" which if true would indeed make Jules Mae's the oldest bar within the Seattle city limits. The problem is that Jules Mae himself didn't emigrate to the U.S. from Belgium until 1892 and the building Jules Mae's is located in wasn't built until 1898. So there's that. Jules Mae didn't even become a co-owner until 1903, and the place wasn't even named Jules Mae's until 1928.

Regardless, it's still a fine old place that's particularly popular with the punk and rockabilly crowd. And you can still find fully functioning pinball machines. I, however, wasn't interested in playing the silver ball, I was there for the pork chops, which, if I may say, are outstanding.

True to Astrid's warning I took it easy on the hooch until she got there so I would be clear-headed and ready to crack the code. She waltzed in, make a quick stop at the bar to place an order before arriving at my table, beer in hand. She looked over my half-finished meal. "How're the chops?"

"Tasty as always. What'd you order?"

"The world famous flatliner."

The name is spot on. The flatliner is a plate full of tater tots, covered in cheddar and jack cheese, bacon, bell peppers, tomatoes, onions and sour cream. And Astrid will finish the whole thing with no guilt, nor a care in the world.

While I sawed on what was left of my chops she set the note out on the table. She was right, it was the same as the others, neat and tidy and elegant. I chewed, swallowed and looked up at her. "Any thoughts?"

She smiled. "As a matter of fact, I do. What I think is that our clue-meister is, as we both mentioned last time, either getting lazy or wants us to figure these out quicker, because I think I had this one figured out on the drive over here."

"Do tell."

"As you said, there's not much here so the target words are already narrowed down."

"And I'm guessing those target words would be Try, try, try a triangle?"

"Yep."

"And those mean something to you?"

Astrid nodded. "They do."

"So, throw me a bone, here. I just spent three hours in I-5 traffic."

She was thoroughly enjoying the fact that she knew the answer and I didn't, and wanted to make sure I was well aware of that fact. I waited patiently, letting her savor the moment. Eventually she broke.

172

"Back in college, you were never in a fraternity." A statement, not a question. She plowed on. "I, on the other hand, was in a sorority, Gamma Phi Beta. Or as the frat boys called us, Grab a Vibrator."

"Frat boys were cleverer than I gave them credit for."

"They had their moments. Now, how familiar are you with the Greek alphabet?"

"Outside of Alpha and Omega, I'm not."

"Fair enough. Well, there's a Greek letter that's basically a triangle, Delta."

"I'm following you."

"And the clue says, Try, try, try a triangle."

"Okay…"

"It's the Try, try, try that gives it away. Three tries."

I took the last bite of my pork chop, chewed and waited her out. I didn't have to wait long. She was eager to spill it. "There's a sorority at the UW, big one, Delta Delta Delta. Tri-Delts, or Deltas. Three triangles! Get it?"

"I got it. So, you're saying our next clue is at a sorority at the UW?"

"I'm saying our next clue is at a sorority at the UW."

The next morning, well, 11ish, so that's technically still morning, we drove up to UW's Greek Row to see what was in store for us. Normally on a Saturday, this time of year, pretty much everyone in the Greek system is at Husky Stadium for a football game, but the Dawgs were in SoCal to pound on the UCLA Bruins so the streets were a little more active than normal. Located just across NE 45th Street, just north of the campus, between 17th and 22nd Avenue, lie 50 fraternities and sororities. Virtually every building in that neighborhood has a series of Greek letters adorning their front.

We found the Tri-Delt house in short order. A gorgeous, and massive brick Tudor; it looked exactly like you would expect a sorority to look like. And it was busy. The street in front of the house was packed with people. More specifically, women. Once we found a parking spot a few blocks away and hoofed it back, we found out what all the fuss was about. The ladies of Delta Delta Delta were having a fundraiser. But they weren't washing cars or having a bake sale, they were selling a very specific, and unusual product to raise cash: yoga pants. Really. And not just yoga pants, those same cheap ones I was seeing being advertised all over the TV lately. This may not come as a surprise to anyone, but this was genius marketing. If ever there was a market for yoga pants, it's young ladies. And you will not find a more concentrated collection of young ladies than on Greek Row. And it appeared every co-ed on campus was right there at that moment.

I looked at Astrid and said, "How are we supposed to find a clue in this riot?

Astrid put a hand to my chest and said, "You stay here. I'll be back in a flash."

Flash being a very subjective word; she returned after about 15 minutes. I held my hands up in the universal "Well?" pose as she emerged from the crowd. She responded by holding up a pair of yoga pants.

"Really?" I said. "We're in search of a clue and you think to do a little light shopping?"

"Relax, Street. Think about it. The clue from last night was pretty easy to crack. Therefore, the clue-meister wanted us here, at this specific sorority today. Not tomorrow, not next week, today. And what did we find that was slightly out of the ordinary? Yoga pants. By my way of thinking, the pants are the clue."

"Yeah, but every other clue was a hand-written note. This would be completely out of synch with everything else we've found."

"Again, I'm getting the feeling our great benefactor is trying to speed up the game. He's saying, 'Quit messing around and cut to the chase. No more time for penmanship and riddles.'"

"Yeah, but yoga pants are just as much a riddle as anything else. Seriously? Yoga pants?"

Astrid threw up her hands. "What can I tell you? I'm just going on my gut."

"But you don't even like yoga pants."

"I don't have to wear them. I just want to see if there's more to them than meets the eye."

I said, "So why did the ladies of Delta Delta Delta decide that yoga pants were the thing to sell for raising money?"

"The girl I spoke with, Ashley, or Brittney, or something that ended in Y said they were approached by a man several weeks ago, a distributor for the yoga pants, offering them at a deep discount, purely for the purposes of selling them as a fundraiser. The girls jumped at the chance. And apparently it's paying off. They've sold hundreds of yoga pants this morning alone. Made the ladies a lot of money."

"Huh."

"And get this," said Astrid. "They aren't the only ones who're selling the yoga pants as a fundraiser. Evidently, they're being sold on virtually every college campus in town, and everyone's making bank. Seattle U, Seattle Pacific, the community colleges, they're all participating. Get ready to see even more yoga pants than ever. If that's even possible."

"Okay," I said. "It's official; yoga pants are a clue."

Astrid held the pants up and looked them over. "Pretty weird, freakin' clue."

We were just getting ready to bolt when Astrid made a funny face. You know, the scrunched up kind when something dawns on you and you're trying to make sense of it.

I said, "Okay, I know that face. What's eating you?"

She stood, tapping her foot, looking around like another clue might be within sight. "Something just occurred to me. You said Farmer Frank was approached by some guy with an almost too good to be true, money-making product—the fertilizer. Now, college students are approached by some guy with an almost too good to be true, money-making product—yoga pants. Coincidence?"

"Maybe. If not, it would be a pretty strange connection: fertilizer and yoga pants."

"I dunno. Seems a bit too convenient for my tastes. I can't help but think they're tied together in some way. It feels like their connection is yet another clue."

"If it is, like you said, pretty weird, freakin' clue."

Astrid took the yoga pants and went home, while I headed back to my apartment to try connecting the dots. It wasn't more than a couple of hours later when my phone rang and I heard the unmistakable voice of Charlie Can Do. He said he had some pertinent information for me but didn't have time to go over it on the phone. Instead he said he'd courier it over. I knew what that meant. It meant a big fat pain in my butt. I can't stand his courier service. With a normal courier service, you open the door, they hand over the delivery and leave. Easy-peasy. But with the service Can Do uses it's not that simple. I waited around, and braced for the delivery. It showed up about an hour later. You can't miss it because you can hear the delivery guy before you see him. And I heard him now. The motorcycle's guttural sound roared into earshot before the telltale squeal of the tires as it came to a skidding stop. And then there's the music. The organ music, sort of a shuffle, that kicks in right before the knock on the door. I always wondered how he pulled that off. It's not like he had a speaker system on his Harley. I took a deep breath and opened the door to greet the infamous Miss Smith Delivery Service.

I have to think that with a name like Miss Smith that Miss Smith would be a Miss. But for the life of me, I'm still not sure. The ever-changing hair (sometimes a sassy blonde, sometimes a shaggy brunette)—definitely feminine. The helmet that looks like it came fresh off a German SS commando—not so much. What makes me lean more in favor of Miss Smith being a dude is his/her voice. I'll be charitable and say it doesn't exactly conjure up visions of Lauren Bacall. Weird appearance aside, the Miss Smith Delivery Service is known far and wide for one distinguishing characteristic: To get the delivery you have to play this inane game with him/her called, *Is it a hit, or a miss?* It goes like this: He/she tells a joke (always in the form of a question) and I determine if it's a hit or a miss. If it's a hit I ding a bell; if it's a miss I smack the side of an old rusty bucket. If it's exceptionally bad I do something that creates a clanky sound; I usually opt for dropping a hammer. If he/she gets two hits he/she wins, if he/she gets two misses he/she loses. If he/she loses I get to hit him/her in the face with a whipped cream pie. I girded my loins and opened the door. Smitty greeted me in standard form.

"Hey, Snookie-poo!"

I cringed. If only manslaughter wasn't a capital offense. "Hello, Miss Smith, what have you got for me?"

"Ready to play?"

"Sure," I sighed, "let's get this over with."

"Where do you get virgin wool?"

"I dunno, where do you get virgin wool?"

"Really ugly sheep!"

Damn. I had to admit, that was pretty funny, but I couldn't let on. I went ahead with the charade and asked the following question like I was a bored game show host talking to the studio audience. "So, is it a hit or a miss? It is a..." I dinged the bell. "Hit. Congratulations," I said with as much false enthusiasm as I could muster. "Next."

Miss Smith jumped right in with his/her next joke. "Why is it so hard to lift a rhino with one hand?"

"Okay, you got me, why is it so hard to lift a rhino with one hand?"

"You ever tried finding a one-handed rhino?"

Hoo-boy. I smacked the bucket. Clank. "Ooh, a miss. Tough luck. That means you have one hit," I dinged the bell (ding), "and one miss," I smacked the bucket (clank). "Another (ding) and you win, another (clank) and you lose. But right now, you have one (ding) and one (clank), so you're going to need another (ding) and not another (clank) because..."

"All right already!"

I truly did enjoy tormenting him/her.

Miss Smith hit me with his/her last joke. "What was the name of the person who made King Arthur's round table?"

"I dunno, what was the name of the person who made King Arthur's round table?"

"Sir Cumferance!"

I skipped right past the bucket and dropped the hammer. (Clank)

"Ooh, I'm so sorry (I wasn't), that's two misses."

I hit him/her in the face with the pie before he/she could get another word in edgewise. "Now let's have the delivery from Charlie Can Do."

Miss Smith reached into his/her courier pouch and removed a small envelope, which I promptly snatched up. I waved Miss Smith goodbye, slammed the door and quickly tore open the envelope. Inside was a piece of paper, and written in Charlie's unmistakably blocky printing, were three words: *Test pants, please.*

Test pants? The yoga pants? First of all, how did he know we had them? And secondly, how do you test pants?

I called Astrid with this latest bombshell and we brainstormed on how best to approach it. After a few minutes of give and take, and some quick Googling, we came to the conclusion that we needed to take the yoga pants to a textile chemical testing lab. I for one didn't even know such a thing existed. We also knew that we still needed to pay farmer Fred a visit in Fife so we decided to divide and conquer again. Astrid would hit up farmer Fred and I would visit the testing lab. We did a drive by hand off of the pants and we each were on our way.

The testing lab, with the explanatory name, Composition Services, was in a drab, nondescript building in the SoDo District, just a few blocks southeast of Safeco Field, where the Mariner's baseball team plays. A bored looking college-age receptionist glanced up from her computer screen. If I was a betting man I'd guess she was killing time on her Facebook or Instagram page. Composition Services didn't strike me as the type of business that had a steady stream of clientele strolling through the front door, especially on a Saturday. She snapped to and asked what she could do for me. I held out the yoga pants and asked how fast I could get a chemical composition test done on them. She took the pants, looked them over and said they could

183

probably have something for me by Monday. I had no idea if that was fast or not but I figured two days was fair and said I'd be back on the appointed day for pick up.

It was late in the afternoon, creeping up on dinnertime, when Astrid called me with her farmer Fred update. I jumped right to it. "What did you learn?"

"I learned that farmer Fred is a very nice old man."

"Okay, let me rephrase my question. What did you learn in conjunction with what I gleaned from my visit to farmer Frank in Ferndale that might help us figure out what the hell is going on?"

Astrid said, "I learned that frple fodder smells like nothing. I learned that frple fodder tastes like nothing. I learned that frple fodder looks like Styrofoam packing peanuts, and I learned it grows year 'round."

"Tell me something I don't know."

"Okay, how about that farmer Fred's frple fodder has been growing like gangbusters over the past few months."

"Let me guess, he started using a new fertilizer about six months ago."

"Yup."

"Was he wearing yoga pants?"

Dripping with sarcasm. "Ha, ha."

"So, back to my original request, tell me something I don't know."

"Like maybe the name of the fertilizer company?"

"Now we're talking! What is it?"

"Verruca enterprises."

"Verruca? Like Verruca Salt, from Willy Wonka?"

I could hear a shrug in her voice. "Pronounced the same."

I thought on this for a second before asking my next question. "Just out of curiosity, what else does farmer Fred grow?"

"I was wondering when you'd ask me that. I'll give you three guesses and the first two don't count."

I said, "Pumpkins?"

"Give the man a cigar."

"And let me guess, they were enormous."

"Ding, ding, ding! We have a winner, ladies and gentlemen!"

I nodded. "Good job, babe. Come on home and I'll treat you to a fine home-cooked meal. And by home-cooked I mean a Dick's Deluxe, fries and a chocolate shake."

"How about Canlis instead?"

"Can't afford it."

"Then Dick's it is. Oh, one last thing I found particularly interesting. About the pumpkin patch."

"Such as?"

186

"Pumpkin patches are a big thing this time of year. Moms and dads pack up the kids, take them out to the pumpkin patch, climb on a wagon, sit on hay bales, towed out into the patch by a tractor. Afterward, maybe a trip through the corn maze and some hot cider by the barn."

"Sounds very Norman Rockwellian. Your point?"

"There was none of that at farmer Fred's."

"Hmm. Now that you mention it, it was the same thing with farmer Frank. I didn't think about that, but that is kind of weird. We're already into October and half his pumpkin crop was still on the ground. I would think it would be picked nearly clean by now. And another thing, when I asked about his huge pumpkins, farmer Frank said his client was thrilled. Client. Singular. Stupid me, I didn't bother asking who his client was."

Astrid said, "Luckily, I asked farmer Fred that very question. You ready for this?"

I waited. She waited. Damn her, she was enjoying this way too much. I gave an exasperated exhale, code for knock it off. She acquiesced.

"Drum roll please...." She then made a drum roll sound effect, complete with cymbal crash. "Starbucks."

"Starbucks? Pumpkins?"

"Pumpkin spice..."

The lightbulb went off for me. "Lattes. Got it. Honey, this is getting weirder by the minute."

"As you would say, tell me something I don't know."

The Seahawks were playing on Sunday so that meant I wasn't going to get jack done. I had a date with my couch, my TV, and beer. And chips. Then I'd probably take a nap. Needless to say, the great Seattle mystery took a 24-hour vacation. It's the 11th commandment: Thou shalt not work on Seahawks Sunday. Monday, however, was a different matter. I got a call from Composition Services. The woman on the phone, someone different from the receptionist I left it with, said the yoga pants and a full report were ready for me to pick up. I raced down to SoDo, eager to see what could possibly come from testing yoga pants. As it turns out, plenty.

The woman at the front desk, the same one who called me, handed over the pants and a large envelope. Evidently the report was inside. She asked me if I wanted to go over the report with the technician who ran the tests. That struck me as a good idea so she escorted me through a door into a hallway which led to another door. I expected this would be the entrance to the lab, but once opened I saw that it was merely a small conference room. She told me to take a seat and the technician would be with me in just a moment. I hadn't been seated for more than a few seconds when the door opened and a man walked in. He was a congenial-looking fellow, probably early 40s, thinning hair that once might have been brown, but was now more salt than pepper. He wore a white lab coat and a cordial smile. We shook hands and he took a seat opposite me at the table.

"So," he said. "You're the gentleman who brought in the yoga pants."

"That would be me."

He indicated to the envelope on the table. "Have you looked at my report yet?"

"Not yet."

He paused for a moment, trying to figure out where to begin. "An interesting find."

"In what way?"

"Well, first let's start with what I expected to find. Yoga pants are by and large made from polyester, nylon or spandex. Nylon is the most durable, strong and long-lasting of all sportswear fabric. In fact, nylon was developed to mimic the softness and strength of silk. The real cheapies are made from polyester, which is nylon's cheap knock off that has little of nylon's strength—not to mention that it tends to be significantly scratchier. And who wants scratchy in their yoga pants, right?"

"I can't imagine."

"Right. Now, these pants are incredibly popular right now. I'm sure you've noticed."

"Hard not to."

"Exactly. And this brand, in particular, has been exceptionally popular, locally. You can't turn on a TV without seeing an ad for them. Combine that with the fact that they're selling so inexpensively and, boom, you've got a run on the market."

I looked at the pants and said, "So I'm guessing, since they're so cheap these are made from polyester."

"That's what I would have guessed as well, but no, they're a custom blend of cotton/poly/spandex. High-end stuff. These are the kind of yoga pants you might expect to find at REI or other quality outfitters."

"The makers must be taking a financial bath."

"Probably. Either that or they're simply flooding the market, getting word of mouth and then will eventually jack up the price to their real value."

"Okay, so back to the composition of the pants. What did you find?"

The technician looked excited. He reached over and tapped on the pants. "At first glance, nothing. I found exactly what I would expect to find. But then something interesting happened. I had my water bottle on the table near me and I clipped it with my hand while I was reaching for something. The bottle fell over and a little water spilled out onto my table before I could pick it up. No biggie. Some of the water spread over to where the yoga pants were and they got a little wet. Not much, but a little. As it turns out I'd been using my chemical vapor analyzer just a few moments earlier and I hadn't shut it off. It was just sitting there on the table next to the yoga pants, and when the water hit the pants the analyzer lights up like a Christmas tree and starts beeping.

My antenna started to quiver. "What happened next?"

"So, I check the analyzer and it's getting a reading of a volatile organic compound essentially woven or baked into the fabric."

"What kind of compound? It wasn't something that could be used in fertilizer, was it?"

"No."

(Rats)

"Why do you ask?"

I had to pull a Grinch confronting Cindy Lou Who. I thought up a lie, and I thought it up quick.

"My, uh, wife was wearing the pants while she was doing yard work last week. I wanted to make sure what you found wasn't simply residue from that." Whoo, boy, do I suck at lying. But for whatever reason, the technician seemed to buy it.

He said, "I couldn't pinpoint it, but it was the after effects where things got interesting."

I could see the technician was having a blast with this. Maybe that's why he bought my lame lie. I'm sure most of his work is tedious, boring

192

analyzation with expected results. Suddenly he's got something he wasn't expecting and he's feeling like Sherlock Holmes. I didn't want to seem overly eager so I did my best to look only marginally curious, which, I'm sure killed his buzz to some degree, but he was still clearly amped.

He said, "Are you familiar with SSRIs?"

Believe it or not, I was. My mother struggled with anxiety issues and took the appropriate meds to help counter it. SSRIs are selective serotonin reuptake inhibitors. SSRIs work by enhancing the function of the nerve cells in the brain that regulate emotion. The chemical messengers that deliver these signals are called neurotransmitters. Serotonin is one type of neurotransmitter.

I told him I had a rudimentary understanding, which, I suspect, he interpreted as I could barely spell it. He said, "Once the compound vaporized it basically had the effect of being an *anti*-SSRI."

"Wait, you're saying it became a stimulant?"

"Well, technically SSRI's are a stimulant, but they're a euphoriant; they make people happy. This stuff?" The tech nodded sagely. "A bad stimulant. And at high enough levels, an irritant." The technician poked the pants with a ballpoint pen. "So, what's the story on these pants?"

I rose, muttered something about an article and research, thanked the technician for his time, told him I would get back to him with more information later—which was a lie—and excused myself. The jumbled puzzle just became clearer to me.

When I got to my car I got out my phone and scrolled through my contacts. It's a pretty exhaustive list. Just about every person I've ever called is logged in here. It's something you just do when you're a columnist. You never know when you're going to need to reach someone for a confirmation. I found the number I needed to call and hoped the person hadn't changed numbers in the years since I last spoke with them. I dialed and held my breath.

The person I called answered on the third ring. They didn't seem surprised to hear from me. They agreed to meet me at a designated location at precisely three o'clock. I hung up. The next call I made was to Astrid. I told her what the textile technician had for me and said I had one last stop before I could tell her more.

She said, "What more are you expecting?"

"A complete and total explanation of everything." And I hung up the phone before she could freak out and demand answers.

The Nickerson Street Saloon makes a damn fine burger. They've got lots of outdoor seating and a terrific location. Born in 1995, after two bartenders took over the space, formerly the 318 Tavern, the Nick is located at the southwest corner of the Fremont bridge. I entered and immediately headed to the back "green room" section. It's a space just slightly isolated from the main dining area, and painted forest green. It's a bit cozier and makes you feel a tiny bit more private than the rest of the bar and restaurant. I took a corner table, my back to the wall so I could see the entrance of my guest and began the wait. I was five minutes early so I took the time to get a head start and ordered a pint of Mac & Jack's African Amber. It was after lunch and before the Monday night football crowd so the place was relatively quiet. Only three other tables were occupied at the time, the closest a good 20 feet away, out of listening distance.

At 3pm, sharp, my guest arrived. He swept into the room, like Carly Simon so eloquently stated in her hit song, *You're so vain*, like he was walking onto a yacht. However, his hat was not strategically dipped below one eye, and his scarf was most definitely not apricot. He wasn't wearing a scarf, he wore a cape. And his hat was dipped over both eyes.

Ladies and gentlemen, I present to you, the one and only Boris S. Wort.

Boris spotted me in the back room; he hunched over, draped his cape over his arm, held up just below eye level—again with the Bela Lugosi Dracula imitation—and paraded over to my table. Always the consummate showman. Seeing Boris up close can throw you. He's a larger than life character to be sure, and an imposing presence. Well over six feet tall and broad of shoulder, he fills up a space. But the costuming, the accouterments, can be disappointing. At this distance, the white tee shirt, cape and visored hat have a distinctly cheap look and feel to them. I always get the impression they're strictly for middle-to-long distance affect. Like costumes for a play or opera. From the 20th row, you're only getting the broader picture and everything looks impressive, but on closer inspection, you see the hastiness of the construction. Boris has been crafted to fool people from the 20th row. And it's worked for decades.

He pulled up a chair and flashed a sign at the waitress who clearly knew what he wanted and nodded back her recognition. Apparently, Boris is well known at the Nick.

Boris slouched back in his seat and threw a sneakered foot over his other leg; all of his movements big and exaggerated.

198

"Hello, Boopsie." His affected Eastern Bloc accent still just as strong as ever.

I took a hit of my beer and began the process. "Thanks for meeting me, Boris. It's been a while."

"Yes, yes it has," he replied. "A splendid article. Three-thousand words, if memory serves. Right after I'd become the second meanest man in the world."

"Got to hand it to you, Boris. Great memory. You still doing the good air out, bad air in thing?"

"Every morning, Boopsie."

I glance around, a few more customers having filled tables. Normal people, people living ordinary lives who have never tried changing an entire city's culture, never attempted to alter history. Looking at Boris sitting across from me I'm reminded of the iconic scene in Michael Mann's movie, Heat, where cop Al Pacino and crook Robert DeNiro calmly sit down for a man-to-man chat. I saw myself in the Pacino role and started the ball rolling.

"You've tried blowing up the Space Needle how many times?"

A shrug. "I've lost track."

"You've never gone to jail, which I find remarkable."

"To go to jail you have to be proven to have broken the law."

"You looking to start now?"

"You see me knocking over liquor stores with a "Born to Lose" tattoo on my chest?"

I shook my head. "No, I do not."

"Right. And I have no intention of ever going to jail."

"Then don't take down scores."

Boris glances over at the main room, wondering where the waitress was with his order. "I do what I do best. I take scores. You do what you do best, you write about them."

"You never wanted a normal-type life?"

Boris actually sneered. "What's that? Barbecues and ball games?"

"That's part of it."

"That's nice. That your life?"

"As much of it as I can."

"Bully for you."

The waitress finally arrived with his order. A Guinness, by the look of it. He saw my look. "Goes with the cape. It's all about appearances." He held up his glass and we tapped. Just a couple of fellas.

I took a sip and said, "We're sitting here like regular guys. You do what you do. I do what I gotta do. What happens if I have the goods on you and have to put you away?" I paused to let that sink in before continuing. "I won't like it. But rest assured, I will not hesitate."

Boris gave me an oily smile, took a long draught and wiped his mouth with the back of his hand. "So, tell me Boopsie, may I call you Boopsie?"

"Why stop now?"

"So, what it is that you believe I have done that might be worth a few sad column inches in your dying newspaper?"

I came here to put my cards on the table. I was all in.

"Seattle's vibe has a crack in it," I said. "The crack's widening. I think you're the one who's cracked it. I think you want it to split wide open. I think you want Seattle to lose its charm. It's politeness. It's chill. I think you want Seattle to become New York-west."

Boris simply nodded. "You think a lot."

"Comes with the job. I know what you're up to and I'm going to make sure everyone else knows as well."

Boris propped his elbow on the table, leaned in, setting his granite chin on palm and said, "Do tell."

I smiled back, confident in my sleuthing abilities. I had the goods on him, and regardless of his cool demeanor, I could sense he knew it as well.

"You're a creature of the spotlight, but for some reason you go radio silent for months. Off the grid. Very un-Boris-like of you. Then suddenly, I'm starting to see strange behavior around town. Very un-Seattle-like behavior. I see a few instances, I write them off as anomalies. I see them cropping up on a regular basis, I see a pattern."

He smiled under his sharpie curlicue mustache. "Do you now?"

"I do," I said. "And not only are people's behavior changing, but the resident frple population's has as well. Ggoorrsstt got grumpy."

"How alliterative of you."

"Thanks. It's a gift. According to a certain Ketchikan, Animal Man, frples are pretty cheerful creatures. Suddenly our one and only loses his happy gene. Coincidentally, at the same time I'm seeing wide-spread irritability and attitude around the city. My reporter antenna says something's up, so I start digging. Ggoorrsstt's grumpiness led me to explore the eating habits of frples, which in turn took me to the lands of farmer Frank and farmer Fred. And guess what I found?"

Boris shook his head, clearly enthralled. "I can't imagine."

"I found frple fodder. But not just any frple fodder, I found frple fodder growing at mutant levels. At both farms. Coincidence?"

Boris smiled even more. "I'm thinking, no."

"And guess what? The crops right alongside the frple fodder are growing like crazy as well. And wouldn't you know it, it was all due to an amazing new fertilizer farmer Frank and farmer Fred both started using. What are the odds?"

"They must be astronomical."

"You would think. But apparently some never-before-heard-of fertilizer salesman made a house-call to the two farmers and convinced them that his new product would double their crop output."

Boris raised his beer. "Good on the farmers!"

"I did a little research on the mysterious salesperson. Evidently, he represented a company called Verruca enterprises. Ever heard of Verruca enterprises?"

"I've heard of Verruca Salt."

"Me too. Different Verruca. Know what a verruca is?"

"I'm sure you'll tell me."

"I will. A verruca is a lump that grows on the bottom of your foot. There's another name for it. A wart."

Boris clapped. "Hear, hear. Excellent name."

"So apparently, Boris S. Wort had gotten into the fertilizer business. But why? Normally bad guys use fertilizer to blow stuff up, but this time around, I'm guessing not."

Boris slouches back into his chair. "I abandoned the blowing up game long ago. Too risky. I've got a retirement to prepare for."

The dude was a cool customer, I'll give him that. I hit him with the next salvo. "So how does a certain local villain, with no scientific or chemistry background suddenly come up with some super fertilizer?"

Boris was all ears. "I can't wait to find out."

"I figure he's got a silent partner. One who's got a background in that type of stuff. Or maybe, even a background in darker arts. I'm thinking maybe the fertilizer isn't made by normal means. Maybe it's cooked up using otherworldly methods."

Boris steepled his fingers, tapping them together in mock excitement. "How deliciously unrealistic!"

"I know, right? But realism doesn't always factor in when you're buddies with a witch. A witch named…Zenobia (gasp). And wouldn't you know it, Zenobia (gasp) was spotted by Gertrude at Uwajimaya doing a little light shopping, picking up who-knows-what."

"Maybe she's taking a Szechuan cooking class."

"Don't think I didn't think of that! But I'm guessing you got Zenobia (gasp) to craft some dark arts recipe that, when ingested, made people irritable, cranky, or even worse, direct!"

"Sounds lovely. So how would someone get people to ingest this miraculous elixir? And not just a few people, but vast numbers?"

I sat back in my chair a bit. This was the good stuff here. After a long slug of my beer… "I gotta hand it to you, Boris. It was pretty ingenious. You were really looking at the long con here. You spend months working up your plan, that's why you disappeared for so long. You were mapping out every step. Once you figured out the timing, then it was the execution. You brought Zenobia (gasp) on board and she makes the compound."

Boris held his Guinness up, inspecting it. "I would think a witch would probably call it a potion."

"Okay, fine, the potion. But like you said, how to get huge amounts of people to eat or drink it without knowing it?" I slowly shook my head with admiration. "And here's the genius part of your plan. You weren't selling your fertilizer to farmers Frank and Fred to increase their frple fodder crop, that was simply an unintended consequence. You were selling it to them to increase their other crops. Specifically, pumpkins! And little do most people know that farmers Frank and Fred are the main pumpkin suppliers to Starbucks. So, here's Starbucks, buying all these potion-laced pumpkins, and here's the Seattle population unwittingly slurping up pumpkin spice lattes by the boatload between September and November."

Boris looked on, clearly impressed. "Wow, that's pretty ingenious. The person who must have come up with an intricate plan like that must be a genius."

"Oh, he must be. And it gets better. So, a huge percentage of the local population is cluelessly chugging down your potion, but I'm guessing a super-villain like Boris S. Wort, the second meanest man in the world, and a man bound and determined to become the first meanest man in the world, doesn't want to leave anything to chance, so he has a back-up plan. He wants to make sure as many people as possible are exposed to Zenobia's (gasp) magic potion, so he doubles down on the method of transference. If there's anything more prolific than pumpkin spice lattes in the Seattle area, it's yoga pants. I gotta tell you, Boris, selling the potion-laced yoga pants at bargain basement prices was genius, you even got Amazon—and sorority girls—to help you infect the masses."

Boris looked on with wonder. "And you figured this all out on your own."

I gave a nod, with no small measure of pride. "Granted, the yoga pants thing took me a while to figure out. It wasn't until I had them analyzed that I understood how you did it."

"And how was that?"

"The compound/potion/chemical/elixir…"

"Ooh, elixir, I like that."

"Whatever you want to call it, was basically inert, virtually undetectable when the pants were dry. But funny thing about people who use yoga pants, they often sweat. Or they get rained on. Either way, the moment moisture enters the equation the potion gets activated, vaporizes and is either inhaled or enters the wearer's biology through the skin. And voila! Even more of the masses, subtly zombified to alter Seattle's vibe."

I settled back in my chair, smug as a bug in a rug.

I expected defiance. I expected denials. Or maybe gloating. I expected typical Boris over-the-top theatrics. What I got instead, from the man sitting across from me, was...

"So sue me."

Long pause.

Finally, from my mouth, "That's it? That's all you got?"

Boris took a long hit of his Guinness and held up his free hand, sort of a, *Yeah, whatever*, gesture.

I was stunned. I honestly wasn't prepared for this kind of reaction. I was all ready to go at it, toe-to-toe with the great Boris S. Wort, and he completely kneecaps me with complete and utter indifference.

"So, you admit it? You admit to everything I just explained? The poisoning of hundreds of thousands of people against their will?"

Boris offered a bored shrug.

"You'll go to jail!"

"For what? Poisoning people? You have any idea what it was Zenobia (gasp) whipped up? Neither do I, but if you know anything about

Zenobia (gasp) there wouldn't be a single artificial ingredient in it. The woman's a health nut! She eats millet for breakfast, and throws back fish oil tablets like they're Flintstones chewables. Whatever she cooked up will test pure as the driven snow compared to what Monsanto puts in your pantry."

Boris paused. "Not that we did anything, mind you." He settled back in his chair and gave a slight chuckle. "Give it a rest, Boopsie, you've got nothing and you know it."

I was speechless. I was literally void of speech. I sat there with a slightly stupid look on my face, my mind racing, trying to think up something clever to say. The best I could come up with was... "Oh yeah?"

He matched me with an equally pithy response. "Yeah."

"But it's going to fail, Boris, because I know." I started scrambling for self-assurance, but my voice came out shrill and desperate. "I know what you did and I'm going to write the mother of all articles on it. And once people are wise to your ways they'll stop drinking those pumpkin spice lattes. They'll stop buying those yoga pants. Your plan is going to grind to a halt before Seattle's vibe gets truly altered. You're finished."

Boris laughed that maniacal laugh of his. "Sure. Fine. Let them stop drinking the lattes, let them stop buying the pants. Be my guest. Like you said, a super-villain like me, the second meanest man in the world, a man bound and determined to become the first meanest man in the world, doesn't want to leave anything to chance, so he would have a back-up plan." Boris leaned in on the table. His dark eyes peering at me through the cut-out holes in his hat's pinned on cowl. "You think I didn't plan on this? You think I didn't expect someone to figure things out? This is simply all part of my grand scheme. You don't get to be the first meanest man in the world by taking chances."

My veins filled with ice water. "What are you going to do?"

Boris hit me with the maniacal laugh again. "I'll tell you what. You did so well figuring things out, I'll give you a hint. Makes it more interesting. If I can't get Zenobia's (gasp) potion to the masses through the lattes and yoga pants anymore, I'll need another device. One that won't miss anyone."

And with that, Boris finished off his beer with a flourish, he fished a ten-spot out of his pocket, tossed it on the table and stood up with a stretch. "Remember, Boopsie, it's your word against mine, so bring your A-game. You're going to need it."

Another maniacal laugh—damn it was effective—and he swept out of the room in a flurry of evilness.

Astrid met me at my apartment and found me sprawled on the couch, staring up at the popcorn ceiling. After my meeting with Boris, I needed a little TLC and quickly called her up. She walked in, saw me on the couch, tossed her purse on the coffee table, planted her fists on her hips and said...

"You knucklehead."

So much for TLC. I tried my best to look equal parts crestfallen and determined but clearly failed on both parts. It was clear I was throwing a pity party and Astrid was having none of it.

She shook her head. "Where's your brain? You think you can ambush Boris S. Wort? The man's eaten sharper guys than you for lunch." She grabbed a chair, spun it around so the back was facing me and sat down, her legs straddling the back. "He's made a career of evil, and you thought you'd outmaneuvered him, that you outfoxed the fox?" Astrid threw up her hands like she was adhering big, bold invisible text to the air. "News flash! Reporter gets ass handed to him by super-villain! Film at 11!"

Astrid slouched in the chair, like a seal had popped and all her air was being released. She was finished with her broadside. Well, almost. "So now what, genius?"

Good question. Now what? I'd been so focused on feeling like five miles of bad road that I hadn't really given much thought as to what next. And said as much. "Dunno."

Wrong answer. Astrid buoyed right back up to full strength. "Dunno? That's all you've got? She grabbed the top of the chair and leaned back. I could hear her taking a deep breath, like she was trying to compose herself. She pulled herself back to full upright position and fixed me with a stare that could split an atom. "Here's what you're going to do. I will give you the rest of the day to feel like a complete and total loser, after which you will get back on the horse and finish the job."

And just like that, she was on her feet, purse in hand, across the floor and out the door. I stared at the popcorn ceiling and took full advantage of my complete and total loser window of time.

I knew Astrid and I would be on the outs for a while. I fully intended to take more than a day to feel sorry for myself, and she knew it. She was not one to suffer fools, nor grant pity parties. She gave me my space I and I gave her hers. And that was fine by me. I knew the main reason she was mad at me was because I confronted Boris without taking her along for the ride. And she was going to make me pay.

I used the time to keep up my investigation, but I did it on the QT. I also went back to work. Like, my actual full-time job. The editor was getting antsy and had column inches to fill. Over the next couple of weeks, I wrote columns on run-of-the-mill issues: Seattle traffic = bad. Indian summer = good. The new Seahawks' rookie who plays a mean accordion = damn! In other words, I was mailing it in, and I knew it. It was driving me crazy that I couldn't spend every waking moment trying to crack this stupid case with Boris. When I wasn't working on a column I was doing research. After two weeks, I didn't have a single new lead. The clue-meister had gone dark, my normal contacts made no contact and everything was eerily quiet. The yoga pants commercials were still airing like mad. The Analog even did a piece on the brand's remarkable popularity. They were clearly all the rage. Pumpkin spice lattes were still ubiquitous; you couldn't throw a rock without hitting someone drinking one. And the effects were everywhere, if you were paying attention. I can't tell you how many times I saw people throwing their recyclables in garbage cans, or popping umbrellas during the lightest of showers. And I was getting decidedly uncomfortable with all the direct eye-contact I was receiving from complete strangers. I even heard marginally harsh language over minor disagreements. But frankly, I didn't give a rip. I was getting a bad case of the I-don't-cares; a side effect of my feeling sorry for myself for getting bamboozled by Boris. Which is weird, because I wanted desperately to figure out Boris's master plan. In other words, it was all about me. Am I pathetic or what?

Two weeks in and I still had no ah-ha moment so I did what I always do when in desperate need of inspiration: I indulged.

Beth's Café on Aurora Avenue, just ever so slightly northwest of Green Lake, is a Seattle institution. You go to Beth's to eat yourself into oblivion, and they are happy to oblige. They proudly claim to have been serving classic, hearty American diner food since 1954. They were even voted Best Place to Cure a Hangover by Seattle Magazine.

If anything, Beth's is famous for their breakfasts. You can order it 24 hours a day, seven days a week. They serve a 12-egg omelet and "all you can eat" hash browns that are sure to quadruple your cholesterol numbers in no time flat. The reader board out front boasts "Omelets bigger than your freakin' head!" Plain and simple, Beth's serves comfort food, and at that moment, I was in the market. I ordered the Country Benedict, smothered in gravy and served with hash browns. The Six-Fiddy shake rounded things out nicely. Yes, a shake, for breakfast. Chocolate, peanut butter and brownies, if you must know. And it was delish.

The beauty of eating breakfast at Beth's is that the food is so all-consuming that your brain and body go into complete torpor. Like a frog in a refrigerator. And that's all I wanted. A few moments to absorb and reflect. After spending two weeks reliving my ignominy I gained back enough self-respect to start formulating a new battle plan. What was clear was I couldn't go to print with what I had so far. Boris was right, all I had was conjecture and supposition. I really didn't want to get sued by Boris. After reading the full report by the lab I found that the chemical compound in the yoga pants was, as Boris had said, purely organic. Powerful, yes, but nothing illegal about it. Something that basically had the same effect as extreme caffeine. Sort of like an organic version of drinking a half-rack of Red Bulls. No wonder people were acting cranky.

What was chapping my ass, however, was Boris's comment about how he was going to distribute more of the stuff so everyone would be exposed. Until I knew what he was planning, or how to stop it, the story wasn't complete.

While powering through my several thousand calories of nourishment I played through Boris's clue in my head, just like Astrid and I had done for all the other clues we'd received. He said, another device. One that wouldn't miss anyone. So, what could distribute a consumable product that would affect everyone? First question: How does one consume? Three ways: Eating, drinking or breathing. Boris had already tried the drinking route with the lattes, so my gut told me he was going to go in a different direction. Eating? What could he put the potion in that everyone would eat? A Dick's Deluxe? Didn't seem feasible. That left breathing. So how do you get something in the air so everyone would breathe it? How do you get massive aerial dispersion? Crop dusting? No, that didn't seem right. A plane would have to make hundreds of passes to cover the greater Seattle area. Too easy to spot. To get the product in the air Boris would have to first vaporize it so it could really spread out. The question still remained though, how would he get it in the air? Seattle has a land area of 83.9 square miles. To cover that much ground, you would have to get some serious altitude. But how?

I hit the bottom of my shake with a profoundly loud and satisfying suction sound. After footing the bill, I stepped out onto the Aurora avenue sidewalk and looked up at the autumn sky. Five miles above me a jetliner was leaving a slow vapor-trail across the sky. And that's when I got hit with the mother of all "Duh" moments.

"Boeing."

"Boeing?" Said an exceedingly dubious Astrid.

"How else is Boris going to get the chemical in the air?"

After breakfast, I called Astrid and was able to convince her that I had come back to my senses and was ready to kick ass and take names. She joined me on the west side of Green Lake, by the old Bathhouse Theater. The path around Green Lake is 2.8 miles, which gives a person, or persons, plenty of time to stroll and talk, which Astrid and I used to its fullest extent.

Astrid posed the obvious. "So, you're saying Boris S. Wort, a known character of dubious moral fiber, has somehow convinced Boeing to let him load up one of their planes with a questionable substance, only to rain it down upon an unsuspecting northwest population."

"Well, if you put it that way…"

"That's the only way to put it, you rockhead!"

I said, "He is a master of disguise. He fooled farmers Fred and Frank with his fertilizer salesman bit, and the sorority girls, too."

"Fooling a couple of bumpkin farmers and some cheerleaders is a far cry from pulling the wool over the eyes of rocket scientists and aeronautical engineers!"

She had a point. "So how else would he do it?"

Astrid went quiet for a while as we passed the amphitheater grandstands that used to house everything from the Aqua Follies to Led Zeppelin. The concrete structure, much smaller than in its heyday, was built in 1950 for the very first Seafair and was called the Aqua Theater, where every summer from 1950 - 1965, 5,200 seats would be filled to watch "swim-musicals" and other water-based entertainment. The star attractions were two groups of female performers: The Aqua Dears, who did a sort of synchronized swimming thing, and the Aqua Darlings, who did I'm not sure what. The theater's swan song was a 1969 concert by, yes, Led Zeppelin.

After we'd passed the structure Astrid stopped dead and turned to me with a snap of her fingers. "A private party."

"What do you mean?"

"I mean I think your idea of an aerial distribution is spot on, but not through Boeing. It would have to be through a smaller organization or a single individual."

Astrid seemed energized by this revelation and began walking again, much faster. I double timed it to keep up. She said, "You know how all these rich dudes like Jeff Bezos and Elon Musk are starting their own space exploration companies, trying to privatize space travel? Same thing. I think Boris has found a deep-pocketed partner who has aerospace connections."

"So how do we find this rich silent partner?"

"Who knows everyone in this town? Who is drawn to Seattle's well-heeled hoi polloi like a moth to flame? Who thrives on basking in the reflected glow of Seattle's movers and shakers. Who is the master of networking and relationships? Who knows how to work a room like nobody's business?"

Only one person. "Gertrude."

I could tell Astrid was glad to be back in the game. She was practically giddy at the prospect of seeing what Gertrude might know. I put in the call and Gertrude said she was more than happy to meet. She told me to swing by her condo and she would answer all my questions. After I hung up it occurred to me that I'd never actually seen where Gertrude lives before. The thought boggled my mind. What kind of place would Gertrude call home? I couldn't even begin to guess. But once I looked at the address it gave me a good idea: Market Place Tower.

The Market Place Tower is a level of swank above filthy rich swank. Six months ago, I did a column on the ten most expensive condos in Seattle that were on the market. Two of the top ten were in this building. Anywhere between four and ten million. For a condo. And Gertrude lived there? I had to see this for myself.

Lesson one about the Market Place Tower: One does not simply walk into the Market Place Tower. At least the living spaces. You see, the Tower only has seven condos, and ain't none of them cheap.

Once we were surveilled, escorted, and buzzed through, Gertrude met us at her front door, arms and smile wide and waiting for us. "Stewart, darling boy, how good to see you!" Her eyes did a quick dart to Astrid and her smile pulled a momentary freeze. Clearly, she wasn't expecting me to be bringing a guest, especially a female one. Gertrude loves being the only woman in the room. Her eyes gave Astrid a once-over and she powered through, her smile still pasted on tight. "And who is your delightful... friend?"

"Gertrude, Astrid. Astrid, Gertrude. Astrid works for the paper and has been helping me on the story."

Astrid returned Gertrude's over the top grin and reached out to shake her hand. "Pleasure's all mine, Gertrude. I've heard so much about you over the years. And it's clear the reports I have received simply do no justice."

Nothing works better on Gertrude than well-timed compliments—real or perceived—and Astrid's words had the desired effect. Within seconds we were swept into the foyer and the grandeur that was Gertrude's domicile.

Allow me a moment to lift my jaw off the floor and try to give you even a sense of what lay before me. The twirling staircase took us up, under a half-dome skylight, to the second level. The views looking west were breathtaking. Nothing between you and Puget Sound. Hardwoods abounded, naturally, and the walls were all in cream with moss-green highlights. The artwork, and there was a lot of it, was of a classical bent. For a woman who wears hand-me-down frocks and combat boots, the décor was spectacularly unexpected. The one thing that did seem on target, however, were the framed playbills. Dozens of them, hanging on walls or sitting on shelves and end tables. And every one of them from a production that Gertrude starred in at some point in her life. I couldn't help but think of Gloria Swanson in Sunset Boulevard; the aging silent film queen who refused to accept that her star has faded.

Gertrude broke the spell and bade us sit on an ornate couch, that would have looked right at home in an episode of Downton Abbey. Sinking in, I looked it over and said, "Nice davenport, Gertrude."

Gertrude was all smiles. "You like it? It's a Lexington Salon sofa. Kiln-dried wooden body with a consistent moisture content that is close to six-to-nine percent. I picked it up on auction at Sotheby's."

She rearranged her dress and crossed a booted foot over her knee. "So, tell me how I can help."

Astrid and I shared a glance before I jumped in. "To be honest, Gertrude, we're not sure if you can or not." I then proceeded to review everything we'd been through since our last chat, including my humiliation at the hands of Boris, and his damning clue about how he was planning on dispersing Zenobia's (gasp) potion.

Gertrude listened patiently, which is saying something for Gertrude. When I finished, she said, "So you're looking for a major player in the aeronautics game who you think will help Boris spray Zenobia's (gasp) juju juice all over creation, yes?"

"Yes."

Gertrude thought on that for a moment before saying, "I think I might know who that might be."

Astrid and I sat up straight, and in unison, "Who?"

Gertrude gave a coy smile and a backhand wave, sort of a *No biggie* gesture. "Quiet fellow. Very well to do. Seems to have his fingers in just about everything these days. He's been silently backing all sorts of projects throughout the city for decades. Not a fan of publicity though. Prefers to keep things on the down-low, if you know what I mean."

I could barely contain my excitement. "Who is he?"

Gertrude gave a coquettish tip of her head. "I'm not at liberty to say."

"Well then, how can we contact him?"

"You can't."

"What do you mean, we can't? This is hugely important! Someone has to find out if he's aiding and abetting Boris with his master plan!"

Astrid jumped in for the first time. "And stop him!"

Gertrude leaped to her feet. "Tell you what. I'll put in a call to him myself. See what I can find out. If there's anything there I'll let you know. Deal?"

Astrid and I looked each other dejectedly. It was clear this was the best we were going to get out of Gertrude. I gave a shrug, extended my hand and said, "Deal."

I fussed and fumed for the rest of the day. Astrid quietly let me vent my spleen and recommended a high ball at the Walrus and the Carpenter in Ballard to take the edge off. I whole-heartedly took her up on the offer.

We weren't halfway through our cocktails when my phone vibrated. I picked it up. "Hello?" I silently mouthed to Astrid that it was Gertrude and began listening. After a couple of beats, "Uh-huh? Really? Hmm. Okay, thanks for checking, Gertrude. See ya 'round." And I hung up.

Astrid said, "Well? What did she say?"

"Gertrude says she can't reach her mystery man. He's gone quiet."

"So, we're back to square one."

"So it would seem." I took a hit of my bourbon and seven. "Nuts. I thought for sure Gertrude would point us in the right direction. What do we do now?"

Before Astrid could even speak our waitress came by and said, "Mr. Street? A letter for you. Someone just dropped it off." And she handed me the small envelope. It was just like the clues we'd received in the past.

I looked at Astrid, and she looked right back at me and said, "Open it up, dummy!"

I quickly tore it open and withdrew the card from inside. It was clearly from our clue-meister. The handwritten script was the same. Astrid said, "What's it say?"

"It says…" And I stopped. I looked up at Astrid and said, "You're not going to believe it."

"What? What am I not going to believe? Spit it out, already!"

I shrugged and continued reading. "It says, *Get your ass over to the center of the universe, pronto!*"

I set the card on the table. Astrid looked at me, and said, "No it doesn't," and snatched it up. She read it aloud. "Get your ass over to the center of the universe, pronto!" She then looked back at me. "Seriously?"

We both scanned the room for our waitress and yelled at the same time, "Check!"

With the adrenaline pumping through our bodies at that moment we could have sprinted to Fremont quicker than it would have taken us to drive, but driving seemed the more reasonable approach. Five minutes later we again, shockingly, found a parking place relatively close in and jumped out of our car, making a beeline for the Center of the Universe guidepost.

The guidepost, located at the intersection of N. Fremont Ave. and 35th St. N. is a multi-colored sign with arrows pointing off in all directions, indicating points of interest and distances to reach them. Among them, the Milky Way (69 light years), the Guggenheim (2653 miles) and the Interurban trail (one block). We stood there, panting, looking this way and that, hoping to spot something or somebody that could clue us in on what was going on, but the place was eerily deserted. Not something you normally encounter in Fremont in the evening. Then, suddenly from behind us… "Hello, Boopsie."

We whirled around, and out of the shadow of the Fremont Rocket that I saw being worked on weeks earlier, stepped Boris S. Wort, the second meanest man in the world.

"Boris! So, you're the one who's sent us out here!"

Boris said, "I have no idea what you're talking about. But I'm glad you're here. I'm glad that you, of all people, will be able to witness my greatest achievement!"

Boris was getting into the moment. He hunched down and, with a wave of his cape, strode forward several steps. It was then that I could see he had something in his hand. A small metallic box, and it had one large red button right smack in the middle of it. Boris pulled up about half way between us and the rocket.

"I told you I had a way to get the potion out to everyone, and now you will get to see it, up close and personal." With a theatrical spin, he held his hands up high in the direction of the rocket. "Behold! The Wort Warhead!"

Astrid and I stole glances at one another. Astrid spoke first. "Uh, Boris, I hate to tell you this, but I think you're off your freakin' nut."

Astrid always had a way with words.

Boris replied with his maniacal laugh. "No, this," he indicated to the rocket with a sweep of his arm, "this is the apex of my master plan. The zenith of years of careful consideration and execution. The peak…" He paused, trying to come up with another clever way of saying that this was the best of his best. He started snapping his fingers and rotating his other hand in an unspooling motion, trying to will the words out of his mouth. "…of, uh, my proficiency. The pinnacle of, um, oh heck…"

I actually felt for the guy. He was killing his moment. He clearly should have rehearsed his monologue. Luckily, Astrid came to his rescue. "Your crowning achievement. The opening cut off your Greatest Hits album. A Boris S. tour de force."

Boris looked at me and jabbed a thumb in Astrid's direction. "She's good."

I couldn't take any more of this. I said, "Dude, the rocket's a shell. It's just for looks."

Boris snapped back into character. He said, "The perfect shell! My crack team of Boris Buddies has been working for months filling it with the necessary hardware and software to take it to a cruising altitude of fifty thousand feet before releasing its precious payload of Zenobia's (gasp!) potion!"

"Wow, that's some good alliterating, there, Boris. But I'm with Astrid, I think you're looney."

Boris smiled his evil, oily smile. "My deep pocketed partner didn't think so. In fact, he's the one who convinced me it was doable. And it is! And you will be here to witness it!"

I said, "Dude, I jump in the air and I'll have longer hang time than that piece of junk. It's a hollow metal tube."

Boris hit me with the maniacal laugh and said, "And a computer is a hollow metal box, until you fill it with the necessary components. And this..." He spun balletically—his cape hung the air for an eternity; he must have a new fabric softener—and pointed to the rocket. "...is jam-packed with the most state-of-the-art aeronautical engineering software available. This will make the stuff they're launching at SpaceX look like wind-up toys."

I hated to admit it, but Boris was selling it. I've seen TED talks less compelling. I also knew I needed more answers. I said, "So Boris, I know you're dying to tell me. Who's your silent partner? Who was nutty enough to buy into your crazy plan and willing to cough up enough money to put a rocket into low orbit?"

"For me to know and you to find out."

"C'mon, Boris. Throw me a bone here. Gates?"

Boris said, "Are you kidding? I needed somebody evil, Gates is busy saving the world from polio."

"Well he has to be local, and the list of local bazillionaires is short. Paul Allen?"

"Go fish."

"Bezos? Anyone crazy enough to deliver goods by way of drone might be crazy enough to go along with your insanity."

Boris nodded at this. "A good guess, but wrong."

"Howard Schultz? You already weaponized his coffee. And he did sell out the Sonics, so as far as evil goes..."

"I like where your head is at, but you're still wrong. And you'll never guess. My man is the master of staying out of the spotlight. He's financially backed more local deals than the other four guys you mentioned, put together. He could buy the Space Needle with what he might find under his couch cushions. The man's a player, and more importantly, he understands what I'm trying to accomplish, and is completely on board. We're of the same mind, he and I. Kindred spirits."

I couldn't, for the life of me, figure who he was talking about. I tried to think of something else to ask but at that moment Boris turned back toward the rocket, glanced over his shoulder in my general direction and shouted, "Ready, boys?"

I looked around, not sure if he was speaking to me, considering Astrid was at my side, and didn't even remotely resemble a boy. Then I saw who Boris was talking to. Two young hipster dudes with cameras. Boris Buddies. Worse, Boris Buddy filmmaker wannabes. Probably straight out of the Seattle Art Institute, looking for a project to make their mark, after their independent shorts got laughed off by all the film festivals. One was working his camera, hand-held, while the other guy was using a tripod. The tripod guy, the one with the ponytail and soul-patch, yelled back, "Ready, Boris!"

It was at this moment I realized I'd completely underestimated Boris S. Wort. Again.

Everything immediately went into slow-motion. I spun back around toward Boris. As fast as you can in slow-motion, and screamed, "Noooooooooooo!" And began a dead sprint toward him. The distance I needed to cover was somewhere in the neighborhood of twenty feet. Under normal circumstances, I could cover that ground in about three seconds, but since I was moving in slow-motion it took decidedly longer. Luckily, Boris was working under the same half-speed working conditions as myself, so it all evened out in the end. The problem, however, is it doesn't take three seconds to push a button. Which Boris did.

I'd only covered about half the distance when the earthquake hit. At least what passed for an earthquake in my ears. The ground rumbled like the great Nisqually quake of 2001, and a tremendous flash momentarily blinded me as a burst of fire and smoke exploded from the base of the rocket.

Something hit me from behind and I fell to the ground. I quickly realized it was Astrid who had tackled me. We both looked up in awe. What we witnessed, we both knew would be burned into our minds forever: Boris, an inky, black shape, arms raised in triumph, his cape billowing around him, silhouetted against the sunburst orange and blinding white of the smoke and flames pouring out of the base of the rocket. The heat from the ignition turned the world into a warped, rippling scene from Dante's Inferno. The only thing missing were prancing imps with pitchforks. Even through the earsplitting thunder of the rocket's engines, I could still hear Boris's maniacal laugh. The man could project.

Astrid and I held each other and squinted into the horror before us, waiting out the last few seconds before lift-off. We waited through the teeth-rattling rumble, expecting a final burst of flame before oblivion. And waited. Finally, an enormous blast of smoke and fire belched forth from the rocket base, knocking Boris flat and obscuring our vision. We were surrounded by a world of swirling smoke. You couldn't see your own hand if you'd held it in front of your face. But what we could do is hear. And what we heard was the thunderous rocket engine coughing and sputtering like an Edsel with a clogged fuel line. Which then morphed into something that sounded like a fifty-foot cat coughing up the world's largest fur ball. Which finally wrapped up with some feeble crackling and fizzles, like you might hear after emptying a pack of pop rocks in your mouth.

When all was quiet, Astrid and I slowly rose from the ground. The air was thick with the smell of

Sulphur and Saltpeter. We looked up in the general direction of the rocket, while the smoke slowly dissipated. We stumbled forward, coughing and choking, trying to get our bearings and nearly stepped on Boris, who had raised himself into a sitting position, a dazed look on his face. We stepped around him and looked up at where the rocket had been mounted, and lo and behold, it was still there.

We walked a few steps closer to get a better look, still wary, in case the engine reignited. The smoke had cleared enough that we now had a pretty clear view and everything looked as it had before. The rocket had not budged.

From behind us, "What the heck?"

We turned to see Boris standing with his hands on his hips, looking utterly put out. "I didn't pay for this!"

A new sound from the direction of the rocket whipped our attention around in a heartbeat. We looked up to where the sound had come from and saw a hatch in the side of the rocket open. A mechanical arm unfolded and a long banner began to unspool, snapping and flapping from some unseen fan hidden inside the opening. At the same time, lights appeared all over the rocket, so that it looked more like something you'd see at an amusement park. They blinked and flashed in an assortment of colors. It was quite striking. The

238

banner completely unfurled and we could now see what was printed on it. Then, right on cue, music started playing from some playback system rigged into the rocket. It took all of about three seconds to recognize it.

"Ground Control to Major Tom. Ground Control to Major Tom. Take your protein pills and put your helmet on."

Space Oddity, by David Bowie. Somebody had a sense of humor. We looked up at the billowing banner. It read, *Nice try, Boris.* Between the flapping banner, flashing lights and music it really did project a carnival vibe. Who wants cotton candy and a corn dog?

The music then changed. Space Oddity was replaced by something new. "She packed my bags last night, pre-flight. Zero hour, nine AM."

Rocket Man, Elton John. A few seconds later another song cut in. "We had a lot of luck on Venus. We always had a ball on Mars."

Deep Purple's Space Truckin'. This was getting good. The next thing I heard was Boris bellowing. "This is outrageous!" He grabbed me by the shoulders and spun me around. "Who put you up to this? Was it the Clown?"

It probably wasn't the most professional thing to do at the moment, but I laughed in his face. "J.P.? Heck no. I have no idea what's going on, but it's brilliant! You got played, Boris. You got played like a cheap, second-hand fiddle."

A new song kicked in from the rocket. "I told you 'bout living in the U.S. of A. Don't you know that I'm the gangster of love?"

I looked at Boris and said, "Steve Miller. Space Cowboy."

Boris pushed me away, violently. "I know who it is! 1969, Brave New World. I have the album!"

Before I could make a smart remark in return a hand reached in between me and Boris. The hand held a small cream-colored card. On the card, a single word. Although I couldn't quite read it upside down, the perfect penmanship I recognized instantly. Both Boris and I looked up at who was holding the card. It was the ponytail/soul patch guy; the Boris Buddy filmmaker. Except now he carried himself with a quiet professionalism. He bowed slightly and said with exceptional eloquence. "For you, from our employer." He nodded again, turned and strode away.

Boris looked at the card, then looked at me, then back at the card. He said, "What the heck?"

I also looked at the card and said, "What's it say?"

Boris held it out at arms-length. Clearly, he hadn't brought his readers with him. "It says, *'Sucker!'*"

240

I heard a loud snort, and turned to see Astrid peering over my shoulder. She quickly covered her mouth, but the damage was done. Boris looked up with eyes that could ignite wet newspaper, tore up the card and stormed off into the night. The Police's Walking on the Moon played him off.

Most of the smoke had cleared, but all the ruckus had begun to draw a crowd. The nearby bars emptied and the patrons were now roaming about, asking each other questions and taking selfies with the rocket in the background. They would be up on Instagram and Facebook within minutes. Which means my story was aging like unrefrigerated chicken salad. The TV stations would start congregating soon, but I wasn't worried about them. All they'd have are a few drunk eyewitnesses and a whole lot of unanswered questions. I knew I better have something of substance to my editor by morning or some overly ambitious cub reporter from the paper might scoop me. But for some reason, at that moment, I didn't give a rat's ass.

Astrid and I took a seat on a nearby curb and began processing what was turning out to be one of the weirdest nights we could remember. I picked up the two torn pieces of the note and held them together, looking at the one-word insult: *Sucker!* I gotta say, whoever was pulling the strings had some serious brass. Astrid and I looked at one another, looked at the crowd, and, God help us, we started to laugh. Couldn't help it.

And then the helicopter showed up.

Sleek and black. Something out of a James Bond movie. It came swooping in, out of the west and began setting down, right smack dab in the middle of the street, with absolutely no compunction about nearby people, cars or anything. Everyone beat a hasty retreat. Astrid and I just sat there. Couldn't get any weirder, right?

The rotor blades beat a staccato rhythm, slowing to a deeper, thumping cadence. The chopper's side door opened and a stunning woman, dressed to the nines in what Astrid later told me was a Victor Edelstein gown that was worn by Princess Diana in 1985 when she danced at the White House Dinner with actor John Travolta, earning the frock the nickname, "The Travolta Dress". Evidently, before she died in 1997, Shy Di auctioned the dress off for charity, where a businesswoman bought it for a couple hundred grand, making it the most expensive dress ever sold at auction at that time. And here it was in front of me. How the hell Astrid recognized it is beyond me.

The woman walked up to us. She was even more striking up close. Tall, dark features, exotic. And utterly professional. She said, "My employer would like to see you." And indicated to the waiting helicopter.

Astrid and I traded a look, shrugged and followed along. Who was I to turn down a ride in a chopper? Plus, I was dying to know who was the brains behind this caper.

Heads down, we speed-walked up to the helicopter and climbed in. The woman followed. Other than the three of us and the pilot, there was no one else on board. I yelled to the Travolta Dress woman, "Where's your boss?" She simply held up a single finger. Just wait. The helicopter lifted off.

The pilot took us south, over Queen Anne Hill and downtown Seattle. The view was breathtaking. Whenever I see this view of the skyline I can't help but wonder, why would anyone choose to live anywhere else? Seconds later I got an inkling of our destination. We were coming in over Century Link Field; the arches on the stadium roof glowing blue and green. Inside, however, the stadium was relatively dark. It was the neighbor to the south that was more brightly lit up. The chopper banked hard and eased into a hovering descent through the open roof of Safeco field. Within seconds we were touching down just beyond second base.

The stadium was lit up like a home game, but from what I could see, there wasn't a soul around. The M's season had ended a few weeks earlier, again, just shy of the playoffs. Go figure.

The pilot shut down the engines and the rotor blades slowly whirled to a stop. We climbed down and stood near the infield dirt, looking around. The Travolta Dress woman stepped up and said, "My employer will be here in just a moment," and moved back closer to the helicopter, giving us our space. A few seconds later a figure appeared out of the third base dugout. From this distance, I couldn't make him out with any detail. What I could see though was that he was tall and moved with grace and an overabundance of poise. What I wouldn't give for poise. He was dressed in black slacks and a white dinner jacket, complete with bow tie. His salt and pepper hair (more salt) was slicked back, giving him a debonair quality one usually has to watch golden age of Hollywood movies to find. As he grew closer his features became clearer. Funny, he looked a bit like someone I knew. A classier version to be sure, but the man was the spitting image of none other than Leroy Frump.

When he was within a few yards I marveled at the similarity. They could be twins. Finally, he stopped before us and reached out to take my hand, which he then proceeded to shake vigorously.

When he spoke, his voice was the picture of eloquence. He had what was known back in the day as a Trans-Atlantic accent. Somewhere between an English accent and something out of the cultured Hamptons. "My dear boy, I can't tell you how pleased I am that you accepted my invitation."

It was at this moment that all the blood rushed to my head and reality ceased to exist. The man standing before me didn't look just like Leroy Frump, he was Leroy Frump!

A sly, almost embarrassed smile crept over Leroy's face. He said, "I suppose this is somewhat of a shock to you. I'm sorry for the subterfuge, dear boy, but I've found it to be a necessary part of the game, I'm afraid."

Still, no words were capable of coming out of my mouth. Out of Astrid's mouth either, it would seem. We both simply stood there with vapid expressions on our faces. Leroy took this as an opportunity to expound a little more.

"You see, when people think of you as an imbecile, it's so much easier to fly below the radar. I've been living this charade for decades, and I've found it to be most rewarding. It allows me to scratch my performance itch, as it were, playing the simpleton handyman Leroy Frump in public, while behind the scenes I'm allowed to address more pressing issues."

Finally, my mouth caught up with the situation. "You were the clue-meister?"

"Yes."

"You wrote the notes?"

"Indeed."

Astrid said, "Nice penmanship."

Leroy shrugged, a little proud. "The spoils of a classical education."

I said, "And to top it off, you were Boris's silent partner? You convinced him that you bought into his aerial chemical dispersion plan and had the means to make it a reality?"

"Yes, and yes."

Astrid jumped in. "But you double-crossed him."

Leroy smiled at this. "How could I not? That was the plan from the beginning. I had been following his behavior for some time and realized I needed to inject myself into the situation so that I could better control the outcome. Simple business tactic, really."

I could see Leroy warming to the discussion. He went on. "Boris is an entertaining character to be sure. Adds color to the collective, as it were. But he's generally harmless; J.P. has always been able to keep him check, by and large. This plan of his, however, went beyond the pale. I must give credit where credit is due though, Boris's scheme was thorough, well thought out, detailed and achievable. This truly would have been his crowning achievement. I almost felt sorry for the chap, neutralizing his grand ambitions when they were so close to completion. But one does not reach the top spot without besting the best. He'll have to be content with his current station in life."

I said, "You don't really expect Boris to take this lying down, do you? The man's a bulldog. By this time next year, he'll most likely have some new angle."

Leroy smiled broadly. "I expect nothing less and look forward to the challenge."

I thought on all of this for a moment. "So, just out of curiosity, how many other major local events or projects have you quietly been a part of over the years?"

Leroy dipped his head sheepishly and toed the dirt around second base. "I think that's information best left undisturbed, Mr. Street."

At this point the Travolta Dress woman joined us with a leather briefcase. She opened it up and Leroy reached into his inside coat pocket and withdrew an antique fountain pen. Inside the briefcase were papers. Leroy said, "Now, I suppose we should get down to business. I've taken the liberty to draw up standard confidentiality agreements for both of you, in return for, what I feel is a very generous financial package." Leroy looked at both Astrid and me with an almost sympathetic expression. "I know how long and hard you've both worked on this story, and I'm sorry that you won't be able to mention me in it. I trust to your creative writing abilities to find an appropriate way of explaining Boris's publicity stunt. And please know that I completely understand how journalists are not paid nearly their worth. I should know, you are my employees, after all."

I snapped to. "Wait, so you're also the bazillionaire owner of The Analog?

"Indeed. So, I hope you will accept my offer in the spirit in which it is intended."

Astrid and I leaned in for a better look to the paperwork in the briefcase. The only thing that caught my eye was the check and the number of zeros to the left of the period.

"Where do I sign?"

Once the paperwork was complete Leroy, or whatever his real name was, shook our hands and asked if he could give us a lift somewhere. Astrid and I looked around the empty stadium for a moment and I said, "Thanks, Leroy, but I think we'll be okay tonight. We're going to need a little time to process. Plus, we've got a big article to write. Pleasure doing business with you."

Leroy accepted this with a short bow, and he and the Travolta Dress woman climbed into the helicopter as the rotors began to turn. Before lift-off Leroy yelled at us above the rising noise. "You sure you won't join us? We're hosting an event at Benaroya Hall. Violinist Nadja Salerno-Sonnenberg is joining the Seattle Symphony for nothing less than Paganini's Introduction and variations on Nel cor piu non mi sento. I dare say, that should be a most memorable evening."

I'm sorry, but hearing those last two sentences coming out of Leroy Frump's mouth still sounded weird to me. "No thanks, Leroy," I yelled back. "The evening's been memorable enough as is." At which point Astrid and I beat a hasty retreat to the bleachers in time to watch the chopper lift off and head back toward downtown.

We slowly hiked up the stairs to the first level concourse and headed for the home plate stadium entrance, which would let us out at the corner of Dave Niehaus Way and Edgar Martinez Drive. On the way, I used my phone to order up an Uber for the drive home. We walked out of the stadium and grabbed a seat at the base of the Ken Griffey Jr. statue. We sat in silence for a while, until Astrid said, "Hungry?"

"Famished."

"Where do you want to eat? Dicks? Hattie's Hat? Jules Mae's? We're pretty close."

A car pulled up at the curb, our Uber. Astrid and I got to our feet and walked over to the car and climbed into the back seat. The driver, a 30-something guy with pictures of his kids taped to his dashboard, leaned back and said, "Where to?"

I settled back into my seat, looked out the window and said, "Canlis, my good man. Canlis."

Made in the USA
San Bernardino, CA
27 October 2017